Child Care Millionaire

Secrets to Building a Profitable 7 or 8 Figure Child Care Business

Brian Duprey

Published by Child Care Marketing Solutions
PO Box 3107
Crested Butte, CO 81224
www.childcare-marketing.com

Copyright 2018 by Kris Murray and Brian Duprey

All rights reserved. Unless otherwise noted on a specific page, no portion of this publication may be reproduced or transmitted in any form or by any means, electronic or mechanical, including photocopying, recording, or capturing on any information storage and retrieval system, without permission in writing from the publisher, except by a reviewer, who may quote brief passages in a critical article or review to be printed in a magazine or newspaper, or online via the internet, or electronically via radio or television.

First edition 2018
Printed in the United States of America

About the Author

Brian Duprey is a seasoned veteran in the child care business. Along with his wife Carol, they have opened 9 schools over the last 18 years having generated well over 24 million dollars of child care revenue. Brian has opened his heart and mind to write this book to help child care owners and managers create highly profitable child care businesses.

Brian met his wife Carol while they were both were serving in the United States Navy. Following an 8-year Naval career for Brian and a 10-year Naval career for Carol, they decided to move to Maine to raise their children.

Carol started a home daycare to help make ends meet and ran that for a few years before the decision was made to rent space from their church to open their first center. The business grew from there and 8 more centers were opened over the next 18 years.

After their third center was opened, Brian quit his job as a payroll and human resources manager of a large construction company and joined Carol in the child care business.

While building their child care business, Brian and Carol both enjoyed stints of public service to give back to their community. Brian served for 10 years in the Maine House of Representatives and Carol served a term as mayor of their home town.

In an effort to give back to the child care community Brian and Carol have both become John Maxwell certified coaches, trainers, and motivational speakers. Brian is currently a certified child care coach with the largest child care coaching and training company in the world, Child Care Marketing Solutions.

Brian considers himself a businessman and not a master of the English language. This book is a roadmap to child care success and not a literary masterpiece, please do your best to look past any punctuation errors or improper uses of conjunctions, prepositions or determiners.

Acknowledgements

A special thank you to my mom and dad who taught me at an early age that being an entrepreneur was the only way to truly love your boss.

To my wonderful wife of 27 years Carol: The day I married you was the day that I have loved you the least in the past 27 years. My love for you grows each hour that I have been blessed to be married to you. Thank you for putting up with my crazy ideas, and especially for never worrying about money, even when we had a whole lot less than zero.

To my wonderful children Aubrey, Brandy, Angel-LeeAnna, Joshua, and Danae: thank you for teaching me patience. I am in awe of how amazing each one of you is.

A special thank you to my best friend Joel Billings, who gave me a $5,000 loan to help me open my first center.

To Morris Fer, thank you for taking a chance on a couple of young entrepreneurs and investing in our dream.

To Andy Karageorgiou, thank you for financing many of our properties for us. You allowed us to rapidly grow our business without having to borrow money from a bank.

A special thank you to all of the amazing employees I have had in my almost 20 year child care career. I have employed over 600 of the most highly dedicated directors, assistant directors, teachers and substitutes in the world today. I appreciate your hard work and dedication to forming young minds. I am in awe of each and every one of you.

To my amazing co-workers at Child Care Marketing Solutions who helped me with the editing of this book; Sindye Alexander, Katheryn Fisher, and Nina Drumsta thank you so much for your hard work and dedication to the cause of helping child care center owners around the world.

To my amazing child care clients from all over the world that I have coached, thank you for allowing me to help you grow your business.

To my business coach, mentor, and friend Kris Murray, thank you for believing in me and seeing things in me that I did not see in myself. Your faith in me that I could write this book was the motivation that I needed when I would get tired after a long day of writing. I appreciate all of the advice and the editing assistance. Thank you for blazing the trail for child care center owners worldwide to have amazing resources and a mentoring system to help us succeed.

To my Lord and Savior Jesus Christ, thank you for saving me.

Foreword

Quite honestly, I'm not sure where to begin.

I just read the draft of this book you are holding in your hands and I'm a little dazed and marveled by the extraordinary content that lies within.

Before I give you the reasons why this book is going to absolutely change your life (and business) for the better, let me give you the inside scoop about the author, Mr. Brian Duprey.

Brian Duprey is a force. He was born that way. He can't help it. He has pissed people off, said stuff that's not politically correct, put himself out there countless times in the face of being judged, and yet he persists. He doesn't care. Because he is a man on a mission. A mission to help YOU. He is driven by the chance to make a difference in your life, and the person sitting next to you. The people you lead, the families you serve. He will do anything – and I mean anything – to help you if you are his client. He will get in his car in the wee hours of the morning and drive to your home or school if you are down and out. He will get on the phone whenever you need him, to lend an ear or a helping hand. He will tell you the honest truth when you need to hear it, and not sugar-coat it. That's why people love him.

Brian is a fierce warrior. He was born with Osteogenesis Imperfecta, otherwise known as Brittle Bone Disease and he has fought hard in life to get the success he has earned. In marriage, parenting, faith, business, and income, he is successful. Often times, by sheer force of will. His personal motto is "Don't tell me what I cannot do until I have already done it." I couldn't be more grateful to have this warrior on MY team, helping me do battle out in the world every single day – helping child care owners and leaders like you.

Okay, on to the book. This book. Like Brian, it's a force of nature, if a book can be such a thing. This is a no-holds-barred manual to how to be successful. Pure and simple. If you take action on just a tenth of what's in here, you will be unstoppable. From mindset to health to strategic thinking and employee management, you cannot HELP but thrive and get very wealthy if you follow Brian's lead. His exact formula to living your best life of wealth and abundance is laid out here, in 101 principles or "nuggets." Implement these golden nuggets as fast as you possibly can!

This book is a reflection of how we coach and train our clients in the Child Care Success Academy. When you have the "warrior mindset" you start thinking and acting differently than all the other early learning professionals in your region, your state, heck the world at large. We are mavericks. We are renegades. We do the opposite of what everyone else does in the industry. We believe and KNOW that child care can be profitable while being extremely rewarding. One is not at the exclusion of the other.

Child Care can also be a darn tough business to run if you don't run it like a business. If you let your clients and teachers run you ragged, and you don't market hard enough (or at all), you will sadly close your doors and leave the industry with your tail between your legs. This has never happened to any of our current members, and it will not as long as Brian and I are breathing! We take a stand for success and for you. This book is proof of that.

Brian Duprey is helping me lead this mission to impact 1 million children through owners who have better quality, leadership, marketing, full enrollment, and great business practices. Thank you!! And special thanks to our fellow team members and clients who work so hard to help make this mission possible.

Enjoy this gem that you hold in your hands and read it with a highlighter or pen in hand to get the most out of it. Take action one nugget at a time and be further inspired to implement through the client profiles included in this book. They are our proof in the pudding. We hope you will join them soon, and we look forward to working with you!

- Kris Murray

Kris is founder of the Child Care Success Academy and host of the annual Child Care Success Summit. She has written two books: The Ultimate Child Care Marketing Guide and 77 Best Strategies to Grow Your Early Childhood Business.

Kris lives in the mountains of Colorado with her two teenagers Owen and Maeve and her dog Simba. You can learn more about her, Brian, and the team at www.Childcare-Marketing.com

Contents

About the Author .... *iii*

Acknowledgements .... *v*

Foreword .... *vi*

Goal Setting, Mindset & Personal Development *1*

    1. Begin with the End in Mind *3*
    2. Write Down Your Goals and Post Them Everywhere *4*
    3. Read "The Slight Edge" by Jeff Olson *5*
    4. Read Every Day in a PMA Book *6*
    5. Visioning *7*
    6. Join a Mastermind Group *8*
    7. Have a Thankfulness Journal *9*
    8. Focus on High Payoff Activities *10*

Client Profile:
    Summer Picha & Katie Wagoner *12*
    Vernon Mason, Jr. *14*
    Victoria & Andrew Lynch *16*

Make Health a Priority *18*

    9. That "Dirty" Three Letter Word *19*
    10. Vacation Often *20*
    11. Rest Your Brain *21*
    12. Meditate Daily *22*

Client Profile:
    Neydary Zambrano *24*
    Jennifer Vasquez *26*
    Kym Pomares *28*

The Financial Picture *30*

    13. Hire a Good CPA (Not an Accountant) *31*
    14. Know How to Read a Financial Statement *32*
    15. Live Below Your Means *33*
    16. Every Two Years Look for a Better Deal *34*
    17. Have Saving Sub Accounts *35*
    18. Your Center is Full of Used Equipment *36*
    19. Have an Exit Strategy *37*

20. Have Written Financial Goals *39*
21. Make Part Time Care Profitable *40*
22. Have a Scholarship Program *41*
23. Use Fees to Increase Revenue *42*
24. Invest in Your Business *43*
25. Have a Will and a Living Will *44*
26. Don't Step Over Dollars to Pick Up Pennies *45*
27. Manage Your Cash Flow *46*
28. Have a Strict Annual Budget *47*
29. Never Lie, Cheat or Steal *48*
30. Smart Debt Only *49*
31. Pay Down Debt...Smartly *50*
32. Never Pay Credit Card Interest *51*
33. Frugality is Key *52*
34. Credit Cards vs. ACH *52*

Client Profile:
Andrea Wortman *54*
Amber Rogers *56*
Curt & Kathy Gray *58*

Operations *60*
35. Have an Operations Manual *61*
36. How to Work with a Spouse or Business Partner *62*
37. Don't Necessarily Follow a School Model *63*
38. Consistency is the Key *64*
39. Work ON Your Business Instead of IN Your Business *65*
40. Hire a Coach *66*
41. Have an Emergency Plan of Action *68*
42. Use a Phone Script *70*
43. Use a Tour Checklist *71*
44. Create Scarcity *73*
45. Proper Follow-Up *75*
46. Use Technology for Parental Communication *75*
47. Attend a Kris Murray Child Care Success Summit *76*
48. Year-Round Programs Tend to be More Profitable *76*
49. Tracking Metrics *77*
50. Reviews and Testimonials *78*
51. Use 21st Century Advertising Methods *80*

52. Use a CRM System 81
53. Use Hand Written Notes 82
54. Recession Proof Your Business 82
55. SEO: Search Engine Optimization 84
56. Survey Parents Annually 84
57. What Makes You Better Than the Competition? 85
58. Have an Attorney on Retainer 86
59. Licensing Inspectors Are Not the Enemy 87
60. Have a Parental Referral Program 89
61. Mystery Shop Often 90
62. Close for All Hands Training Days 91
63. Have Core Values 92
64. Have an Ambassador of Employee and Parent Happiness ... 93

Client Profile:
Chirag Patel 94
Karla & Doug McCurry 96
Linh Nguyen 98

Management 100

65. Have a Secret Management Facebook Group 101
66. Never Micro-Manage 101
67. Invest in Sales Training 102
68. Develop the Leaders Around You 103
69. Bonus Your Leadership Team 103
70. Develop a "Farm Team" 104
71. Empower Leaders to Make Decisions 105

Client Profile:
Donna Jensen 106
Sharon Foster 108
The Parag Family 110

Employees 112

72. Have a Secret Staff Facebook Group 113
73. Be Quick to Terminate a Toxic Employee 113
74. Have a Social Media Policy 114
75. Get Cell Phones out of the Classroom 115
76. Have a Non-compete and Non-disclosure Agreement 116
77. Treat Employees Right 117

78. Success with Millennials *118*
79. Trust…but Verify. *119*
80. Hire Smartly and Decisively..*120*
81. Reducing Interview No-Shows..*120*
82. Always Audition New Applicants *121*
83. Invest in Your Rising Stars *122*
84. Survey your Staff Annually *122*
85. Have a Staff Referral Program..*123*
86. Set Clear Boundaries *123*
87. Employee Rewards and Incentives..*124*
88. Onboarding *125*
89. Have a Mentorship Program *126*

Client Profile:
Lucy Cook, Bruce Mazey, & Phil Mazey *128*
Sholom Strick...*130*
Lisa Fromen *132*

Expansion...*134*
90. It All Starts with a Decision to Expand *135*
91. Systemize Everything *135*
92. Ensure You are Properly Capitalized *136*
93. Creative Financing..*137*
94. Have a Warrior Mindset..*139*
95. Be the Big Fish in the Small Pond..*140*
96. Think Outside of the Box *140*
97. Use Brokers to Sell, but Not Necessarily to Buy......................*141*
98. Study the Competition *142*
99. Five Centers Are Easier to Manage Than One *142*
100. Patience is Key *143*
101. Recommended Reading...*143*

Chapter 1

Goal Setting, Mindset & Personal Development

I would like you to consider the three following principles: without a goal you will never achieve anything you set your mind to, without the right mindset you will never achieve your goals, without personal development you will never have the proper mindset.

If I had to guess I would say that over 90% of child care center owners are not goal setters and do very little in the area of mindset and personal development. Why is that? Most child care center owners are college graduates, and unfortunately in college today we are taught that when we graduate we have arrived, and the learning stops.

I am not against college in any fashion. In fact, I have pushed all of my children to get college degrees. What I am against is society judging someone for not completing college as if they have committed some cardinal sin. I have read enough books and listened to enough positive attitude tapes to hold a doctorate in mindset and personal development.

I did not graduate college. I took a few business classes while I was in the U.S. Navy, but never saw the point of continuing on. I wanted to be a lawyer but when I found out the salary lawyers made after going to school for eight years and racking up massive student loans, it did not excite me.

What I noticed was that some of the richest people in the world never actually graduated from college, some did not graduate from high school. In contrast, most people who held a college degree worked for someone else making their employer's dreams come true. I knew I wanted to own my own business someday and when I was first introduced to the Amway business in 1990 I jumped at the chance to be in business for myself.

I made millions of dollars in my five years in the Amway business. Of course, Anyway Corporation didn't pay me millions of dollars. However, what I learned in my five years as an independent businessperson for the Amway Corporation helped me

Child Care Millionaire

discover how to make millions for myself.

What I was taught in the Amway business from day one was the importance of personal development, mindset and goal setting. I have been doing it every day since. If you follow the nuggets I lay out for you very carefully, you can build a child care business that generates millions of dollars of annual revenue.

In Nugget 101 I recommend dozens of books that will help you with goal setting, mindset and personal development. I hope you will commit to reading a book or two a month to start reprogramming your brain.

NUGGET #1

Begin with the End in Mind

To become a child care millionaire, you must have a plan to get there. The ancient Chinese proverb says "The journey of a thousand miles begins with the first step." You must begin with the end in mind.

Setting business goals requires you to think ahead. Way ahead. You will want to set these long-term goals.

2-year plan: 2 years from today I will have:

- _____ locations.
- _____ employees.
- $_____ in gross annual revenue.
- $_____ in net annual income.

5-year plan: 5 years from today I will have:

- _____ locations.
- _____ employees.
- $_____ in gross annual revenue.
- $_____ in net annual income.

10-year plan: 10 years from today I will have:

- _____ locations.
- _____ employees.
- $_____ in gross annual revenue.
- $_____ in net annual income.

NUGGET #2:
Write Down Your Goals and Post Them Everywhere

When was the last time you got into your car, turned the key, put the car into drive and had no idea where you were going? When was the last time you planned a family vacation and had no idea where you were going to go?

While many business owners have goals in their mind, very few of them take the time to write them down. Writing a goal down vastly increases the likelihood of accomplishing it, yet many do not do this because they do not want to feel like a failure if the goal is not achieved. Stop being afraid of failure and write down your goals! Write your goals out on index cards and post them on your bathroom mirror, on your computer monitor, across from your toilet. Every time you see your written goals, read them out loud to yourself. The more you see them and hear them, the more your brain begins to believe they are possible.

Here is my 4-step plan to successful goal setting:

- *Figure out what you want.*

    How much money do you want to make, what are your health goals, relationship goals, business goals, personal goals etc.

- *Write your goals down.*

    Take a piece of paper and just start writing things you wish to achieve. Do not be afraid to write down large, scary goals.

- *Be specific and have a timeline*

    "I will weigh 125 pounds 4 months from now" is far more specific than "I want to lose 20 pounds".

- *Have a plan for each goal*

    - Under each goal write a plan for achieving the goal.
    - I will go to the gym three times a week for 30 minutes each.
    - I will eat no more than 1200 calories a day.
    - I will not eat junk food more than one time per week.
    - I will limit myself to one diet soda per day.

Sit down now and write down a long list of your short and long-term goals before moving on to Nugget #3.

Congratulations, you are now amongst the 3% of the population that actually writes down a goal. Having your goal in front of you will allow you to put your plans into motion to achieve what you desire.

NUGGET #3:
Read "The Slight Edge" by Jeff Olson

I have not yet met a child care millionaire who became one by accident. No one ever wakes up, looks at their net worth and says, *"Gosh darn, how did I get here?"*

Mindset is vital to building a successful million-dollar child care business, yet this is probably one of the more neglected areas by business owners.

I read a book 10 years ago that changed my life called *The Slight Edge* by Jeff Olson. This book has fundamentally changed the way I treat each day, how I tackle problems, and how I view the world.

Jeff Olson is a multi-millionaire businessman who has written a book that allows you to gain a very interesting perspective on mindset, goal setting and consistency.

I have spoken to thousands of people throughout my career as a motivational speaker and trainer. Each time I am on stage I talk about how this book has changed my life, and I will continue to do so. You would not be reading this book had it not been for *The Slight Edge*. I used the principles in that book to write this book, and you can do the same in your life.

I suggest that you take a moment right now and visit my website at http://www.childcaremillionaire.com and order this book right now. It will be at your door in a few days, just about the time you are finishing this book. I guarantee that if you read *The Slight Edge* and apply what you learn, it will not be a waste of your time. It will change your life, just like it did mine.

NUGGET #4:
Read Every Day in a PMA Book

PMA stands for Positive Mental Attitude. PMA was first introduced by Napoleon Hill in the 1937 book *Think and Grow Rich*. I highly recommend this book and have included it on my **Million Dollar Book List**.

Positive mental attitude is the philosophy that having an optimistic outlook in every situation attracts a positive outcome.

Your brain is an incredible computer that relies on programming, very similar to a desktop computer. If a programmer programmed a computer to give you the wrong answers to every question you typed into it, the computer wouldn't be at fault, the programmer would be.

You are your brain's programmer, and frankly if you're like the average person, you aren't doing a great job at programming your brain. When was the last time you fed positive thoughts into your brain? Ever heard of the phrase *"Garbage in, garbage out?"*

The average person today will see more useless images in a day than someone 100 years ago saw in their entire lifetime. We are programming our brains with useless garbage day in and day out.

There is nothing wrong with sitting down and watching a television show, and I am not advocating eliminating this from your life. You should make it a priority to spend 15 - 30 minutes each day reading from a positive mental attitude book. By doing this you will totally change your mindset and learn how to tackle problems that you will face as you expand and grow your child care business.

Jeff Olson, in the book *The Slight Edge* recommends reading 10 pages a day. I read that the average CEO reads one book each week. Seeing that the average CEO salary is 475 times greater than the average worker's salary, why do you think that is? In my opinion they are the CEO because they spend their spare time programming their brain for success instead of for failure. To be a child care millionaire you must program your brain for success!

NUGGET #5:
Visioning

Your brain does not know the difference between the truth and a lie. Your brain is a computer, and as we discussed in the nugget on Mindset the programming of your brain is very important.

When you write down your goals, you need to picture yourself already in possession of whatever goal you have set for yourself. You need to tell your brain to picture it in your possession.

Let's say you have a goal to weigh 125 pounds. You need to close your eyes and see yourself on a scale, with the number showing at 125. You need to say out loud, *"I weigh 125 pounds."* Each time you read your goals, you need to read them as if you are already in possession of the goal. This is called visioning, and it works!

Let's say you have a goal to have your child care business earn $1 million this year. You need to repeat to yourself over and over, *"I have a million-dollar child care business."* Picture yourself looking at a profit and loss statement showing $1,000,000 in revenue.

Believe it, picture it, and then your brain will go to work making it come true. It does not know you have not attained it yet, your subconscious will work hard to manifest what you have envisioned.

Your friends and family will think you are a bit looney. They walk into a room and there you are with your eyes closed stating goals as if they are in your possession already.

Do it right now, read each goal that you set in Nuggets 1 and 2 and read them as if you are in possession of those goals right now. This will greatly increase the likelihood of achieving them. Do this each and every day until your goals become your reality. This has worked for me in my life over and over.

"Whatever the mind of man can conceive and believe, it can achieve" ~ Napoleon Hill.

NUGGET #6:
Join a Mastermind Group

In Napoleon Hill's book *Think and Grow Rich*, the author states the importance of joining a mastermind group.

"Mastermind principle is the coordination of knowledge and effort of two or more people who work toward a definite purpose in the spirit of harmony" ~ Napoleon Hill.

I joined my first child care mastermind group in 2015 after I went to The Child Care Success Summit, hosted by Kris Murray, the founder and president of Child Care Marketing Solutions.

I remember vividly going to the conference with very low expectations, mostly looking to have a few sunny days in Orlando with a tax-deductible conference ("mini-vacation").

I was blown away by the conference content and the speakers. At that point I had been in the child care business for over 18 years, and I thought I knew everything about the child care industry and how to run a successful center. That weekend I realized that I had a good business, but not a great business.

Joining Kris Murray's Child Care Success Academy Mastermind Group would prove to be extremely lucrative for me over the next two years. My annual revenue grew by close to $750,000 over the two years I spent in her mastermind group.

Having the power of a mastermind network of other successful child care business owners to bounce ideas off of, share information with, and set goals and talk about your dreams with is amazing. I owe my success not only to Kris Murray for putting together such an amazing mastermind group, but more importantly to the members of the group who gave me encouragement, ideas, files, and documents that helped my business to explode.

The important thing is to find a mastermind group full of child care millionaires and hang around them often. Find out what they know and duplicate it. It is not rocket science.

I personally lead an amazing Mastermind Group of Child Care Millionaires. You can get information on joining my group by emailing me at brian@childcaremillionaire.com.

NUGGET #7:
Have a Thankfulness Journal

Take a moment right now and write out ten things you are thankful for:

1. _____
2. _____
3. _____
4. _____
5. _____
6. _____
7. _____
8. _____
9. _____
10. _____

Was it hard? Probably not. I want you to put this book down, go to an online ordering site, and order a journal.

Each day when you get up I would like you to write one thing you are thankful for in this journal.

There are going to be tough times ahead, it happens to everyone. No one gets through this life without encountering problems. Business owners are hit especially hard with trouble over the course of their business life. Let me show you how to get through those tough patches.

When life hands you a challenge, when you start having negative thoughts, when you start feeling sorry for yourself, when things seem at their worst, it is then time to pull out your thankfulness journal and start reading.

Your brain cannot have a negative and a positive thought simultaneously. By filling your mind with positive thoughts, you will be diluting your brain and changing your mindset. It very hard to feel sorry for yourself when you are grateful.

NUGGET #8:
Focus on High Payoff Activities

Of all of the things you do in a given day, how many of them would you do for free?

To have a child care millionaire mindset, you have to learn the art of delegation. What should you delegate? Whatever you have to so that you can focus on high payoff activities or activities that you enjoy doing.

Whenever you are spending time covering for a teacher, or making lunch, or driving a school bus you are essentially working for a low wage. Your time is worth at least ten times as much as the average employee at your school. Hire someone to do that job you are filling in for, rather than wasting your time doing low payoff activities.

Don't get me wrong, I understand that sometimes this is necessary, especially when your business is small. However, you will never grow bigger unless you master the art of focusing your energy on high payoff activities.

This requires a mindset shift. As you add locations you must add a firewall between you and your staff. That firewall ensures you can focus on high payoff activities.

When I opened my third location I added an executive director position, which freed me up to work ON my business instead of IN my business. This person took over hiring and scheduling from me, so when she was understaffed she knew that she had to be the one covering. This seldom happened. Plus, she knew that my wife and I were off limits as far as coverage, and she had to find a way to make it work.

Not being pulled into day to day operations allowed me to focus on growing the business, spending each day on high payoff activities that generated more revenue. I was able to focus on staff and parent retention, marketing, and social media.

Find a structure in your business that allows you to prioritize your day so that you are spending at least 80% of your time on growing your business, and you will quickly become a child care millionaire. If you keep getting drawn into the daily grind, twenty years from now you will still be driving the bus and making lunch.

CHILD CARE PROFILE

Summer Picha & Katie Wagoner

Peaceful Valley Montessori Academy

Location: Minnesota
Year Opened: 2009
# of Employees: 65
# of Locations: 3
2017 Gross Revenue: $3 Million

How did you finance your first location and what did it cost?

We used a sale lease-back process through a REIT (Real Estate Investment Trust). The building was $1.8 million and the remodel was about $500,000. The REIT financed $300,000 of the remodel. We took out a personal loan for the remainder.

What is the biggest mistake you made in your business in the first two years?

One of our biggest mistakes was definitely lack of signage and pre-marketing!! Another thing we didn't realize was everything costs more and takes longer then we anticipated!!!

What are some of the smartest business decisions you have ever made?

Surround yourself with a team of good people who are experts in their field! Create a team of people you trust and can have on speed dial: an accountant, bookkeeper, broker, business advisors, friends in the industry who can advise you, insurance agent, architect, and others who are experts in areas that you may not know much about.

What advice would you give to someone thinking about opening or expanding a child care center?

We get asked this question quite often. Our work is not for the faint of heart, but it is so rewarding. Making quick decisions is something every entrepreneur has to do. Try to gather as much information as possible to make an educated decision, but DO NOT IGNORE YOUR GUT INSTINCTS! This job is a roller coaster of emotions, the highs are high and the lows are low. During the high times, enjoy - spend time with your family, spend time away from your school/center and do not feel guilty about it!

Thoughts from Summer & Katie:

We are nothing without our team.

CHILD CARE PROFILE

Vernon Mason Jr

WEE SCHOOL Child Development Centers, Inc.

Location: North Carolina
Year Opened: 1991
# of Employees: 125
# of Locations: 5
2017 Gross Revenue: $3.38 Million

How did you finance your first location and what did it cost?

Citibank $5000 credit card. It was leased space so that was our budget to open.

What are some of the biggest mistakes you made in your business in the first two years?

- *Selecting a space that was too small. Do not get locked into a space without room to grow.*

- *Not making timely payroll tax deposits! Ask for help! Do not try and do everything yourself! I began using a local payroll company and my payroll taxes have been done on time for 20 years!*

What are some of the smartest business decisions you have ever made?

Owning my real estate. Wealth can be built multiple ways in our industry.

1. Profits: Wealth can be built if your market allows you to operate with a great profit margin, whether you own or lease your real estate. Some markets are virtually a break-even scenario.

2. Real Estate: Owning your real estate is a long-term payoff. At retirement or when you are ready to exit the industry you hopefully can sell at a profit or lease your real estate for long term income.

What advice would you give to someone thinking about opening or expanding a child care center?

- *More is not always better! I see as many individuals who are very successful with one or two locations as I do much larger multi-site companies. Whether big or small the stressors will remain, they will just be different stressors.*

- *This field is too difficult to live paycheck to paycheck and not to make a "good living." Figure out what is feasible in your market and persevere until you get it right. Know your numbers in a timely manner, if you do not know whether you are making or losing money until months later it is too late to adjust.*

- *Have a business coach or peer group. Many small business owners get wrapped up in the day to mundane duties of the work, i.e.: providing the service, that they rarely look at the big picture much less do long range planning.*

Thoughts from Vernon:

You learn more from your critics than those that compliment you!

CHILD CARE PROFILE

Victoria & Andrew Lynch

First Discovery CDC

Location: Virginia
Year Opened: 2009
# of Employees: 38
# of Locations: 2
2017 Gross Revenue: $1.3 Million

How did you finance your first location and what did it cost?

$120,000 which included start up and working capital for the first 6 months after opening. We got financed privately with an investor. Our first center had minimal cosmetic changes and was a former child care center that recently closed.

What are some of the biggest mistakes you made in your business in the first two years?

- *I did not market prior to opening! Huge mistake! It took months to build enrollment.*

- *Not taking the time to correctly onboard and retain staff and wasting money on marketing that did not work for us. I also would take it personally when staff decided to move on. I have since grown and realized that everyone is not meant to be a part of your expansion or brand.*

What are some of the smartest business decisions you have ever made?

- *Growing the business where I could stop working in the office daily to work on my business.*

- *Getting ChildcareCRM!*

- *Joining the Kris Murray Child Care Success Academy Platinum group to network with other child care professionals. You are not alone and many owners face the same daily struggles as you.*

What advice would you give to someone thinking about opening or expanding a child care center?

Location is key! Take your time and as much as your customers love the brand-new feel of technology they love the stability of your staff more. Invest in your people and in return you may get a few loyal ones that stick around and help grow your business.

Thoughts from Victoria:

Find a way or make a way.

Chapter 2
Make Health a Priority

You spend so much time and effort building a successful business, but cannot take it with you. What is the sense of spending your life building a million-dollar child care business and then, in the end, only your heirs get to reap the benefits of the wealth you've created? In Nugget #3 you learned about *The Slight Edge*, one of the books that has changed my life.

This chapter is the shortest but has the power to make a monumental difference in your life. The four nuggets that follow when taken seriously can help you to live a long and healthy life.

I have not included much on diet; there are a lot of books on the market that can help you there. As long as you eat a balanced diet and burn as many if not more calories than you take in, your food choices do not matter as much. Learning portion control, developing self-discipline, reducing sugar and sodium intakes, and snacking smarter will help you begin to look and feel better.

NUGGET #9:
That "Dirty" Three Letter Word

When I was in my twenties I did it nearly every day, sometimes twice a day. When I hit my thirties, I starting slowing down and dropped to four to five times a week. In my forties it became harder and harder for me to get excited while doing it, but I forced myself to do it at least twice a week. Now that I am in my fifties, I realize that this is super important to me living a long life, so my mindset has changed, and I now do it at least five times a week. Sometimes I can go for up to 2 hours, which is a lot better than I did when I was in my twenties.

Of course, I am talking about that dirty three letter word "gym". Going to the gym has always been important to me, but as I got older (and a lot busier), it became less of a priority for me. As a result, I gained weight, was put on blood pressure medicine, and was more stressed than ever. This is the perfect recipe for an early death.

What good is it to become a child care millionaire only to drop dead of a heart attack before you can spend the money you've earned?

The early nuggets in this book deal with mindset, which is vital to get right first. Without the right mindset, you will never make your health a priority.

Earlier in the book you wrote down your goals; did you add any health, exercise or weight goals? If not, now is time to do this. Even if you are perfect weight, you still need to eat properly and exercise to help maintain the stamina you will need to operate a successful child care business.

Consistency is the key. Working out 15 minutes each day is far better than spending 2 hours working out on a Saturday. Start slow but start now. Start by doing a little bit of exercise each and every day. Get your heart beating faster, sweat a little, and then repeat. For every hour you spend exercising, you will add days to your life. I think that is a good return on investment.

Eating healthy is very important as well. Here are some quick healthy eating tips:

- Limit sodium

- Eat lots of fruits and vegetables

- Limit alcohol consumption

- Snack (healthy) often

- Start each day with a healthy breakfast

NUGGET #10:
Vacation Often

When was the last time you had a vacation that was amazing? One where you relaxed and did not get calls from the office and you were able to unplug from technology.

One of the secrets to my success is that I never go more than 90 days without a vacation. Try it, and it will change your life!

For the past 10 years or so my wife Carol and I have had a relaxation ritual that includes frequent vacations (every 90 days or so) without our children. This has been one of the keys to our successful marriage of 27 years, and our sanity.

Operating a successful child care business is hard. Having a family can be even harder. Proper balance between all of the moving pieces in your life is vital to the balance in your life.

If you have not had a vacation in a long time without your children, head on over to a travel website and start looking around. Write it down on your goal sheet to take a vacation and give yourself a deadline to get it booked.

Vacation rules:

- Do not check in with the office, let them know to only contact you in an emergency.

- Do NOT do any work.

- Trust your staff and whoever is watching your children.

- You may check your phone 2 times a day, but do not have it with you. Leave it in the room.

- Hold hands, rekindle your relationship, have fun and relax.

- Do something totally out of your comfort zone.

Later in this book I am going to show you how to get airline tickets for free, that way you have no excuse for not taking a much needed vacation.

NUGGET #11:
Rest Your Brain

In today's fast paced world our brains are being worked at a faster pace than at any other time in history. Your brain has to process more images in a day than someone who lived 100 years ago had to process in their lifetime. It is no wonder we are constantly tired!

The best way to properly rest your brain is to get at least 7 hours of sleep a night, preferably 8 hours. You may think that is not possible, but I will tell you that it is if you learn to discipline yourself.

When you sleep your brain does not. This is where your brain rests, but it still has to work. While you are sleeping your brain takes things you saw or learned during the day that are in your short-term memory and files them away into your long-term memory.

Improper sleep disrupts the ability of the brain to store the appropriate information and can cause memory problems and other health issues.

Consistency is the key here. Going to bed at the same time every day is very important to brain health. Drinking enough water is also important (your brain is mostly water). Limiting alcohol is also important, as your brain will not be able to properly do its job while you sleep until all of the alcohol is out of your system. Additionally, do not drink caffeine past noon or it can disrupt you from getting into a deep sleep.

In the 27 years my wife and I have been married we have made a pact to always go to bed at the same time, together. We have made intimacy, which is also important to brain and body health, a very important part of our marriage.

Another secret to good brain health, and also a good marriage, is to never go to bed mad at each other. In order for your brain to rest, it must not be stressed. If you have a fight right before bed, your brain will not be able to shut down. As the Bible says, *"Let not the sun go down on your wrath"* - Eph 4:26 KJV.

NUGGET #12:
Meditate Daily

Meditation has been proven to reduce blood pressure, boost your immune system, and help you to live a longer, happier life.

In the previous nugget we talked about resting your brain at night, but I am going to explain to you how to rest it during the day.

I want you to read out loud the meditation process first, then I will want you to practice it. Yes, I do want you to actually do this.

Begin by finding a quiet spot where you will not be disturbed for 5 minutes. Set the alarm on your phone for 5 minutes from now. Place your phone on silent as to not be disturbed.

Close your eyes and count to five as you inhale slowly and deeply through your nose. Then hold your breath for a count of five before you slowly exhale out of your mouth to another count of five.

If the count of five is easy for you try increasing to six, seven, eight, nine, or even ten. Find the highest number that you can breathe slowly and steady with.

Once you have mastered your breathing I want you to start visioning, in your meditation, a happy place. Since your brain can only focus on one picture at a time, we need to create a happy place that your brain can focus on to keep it from thinking about work while you are meditating.

My happy place is a Caribbean beach. I picture myself sitting on the shore with the waves rolling up on my feet. I can smell the salt air, see the blue sky and feel the water.

Now I want you to picture what your happy place is. Use your five senses to smell, feel, taste, see, and hear your happy place. Set your alarm for five minutes and try it. How did it feel? Do you feel more relaxed? Doing this one or two times during each day will significantly reduce stress and make you a happier person.

CHILD CARE PROFILE

Neydary Zambrano

Magic Memories

Location: Pennsylvania
Year Opened: 2006
# of Employees: 48
# of Locations: 4
2017 Gross Revenue: $2.6 Million

How did you finance your first location?

Purchase price was $900,000 for the business and the real estate. I used a combination of personal funds and a conventional bank loan from a small bank.

What was the biggest mistake you made in your business in the first two years?

Not spending money on advertising or marketing. I thought I did not need to because I was near capacity. Another mistake was not seeking mentors and a support system.

What was the smartest business decision you have ever made?

Hiring and training the right staff.

What advice would you give to someone thinking about opening or expanding a child care center?

If you love what you do, expand! Make sure that you get support to help you!

Thoughts from Neydary:

Always know your numbers!

Saving every month should be a must in your program!

CHILD CARE PROFILE

Jennifer Vasquez

A Sunny Start Preschool & Born 2 Learn

Location: Florida
Year Opened: 2012
# of Employees: 49
# of Locations: 3
2017 Gross Revenue: $1.75 Million

How did you finance your first location and what did it cost?

$320,000 = 50% cash down and 50% seller financing. 8% int. only payments with balloon at 2 years.

What is the biggest mistake you made in your business in the first two years?

My time was consumed working in my business rather than working on my business. Rather than hiring a Director, I filled the position to save on overhead cost. However, by saving on overhead I did not maximize on the additional revenue that the school could generate.

What are some of the smartest business decisions you have ever made?

At the time I purchased my second center I was the full-time director in my first center and hired a Director to operate the second center. Within the first 5 months of operation the school was operating at a loss. Regardless of the losses I immediately hired a Co-Director. In doing so this allowed the Director to focus on enrollments in the school. What led me to make these decisions, is the Kris Murray Child Care Success Summit that I attended. Attending this conference and later joining the Child Care Success Academy honestly made me very successful at a much faster pace and perhaps with higher profit margins.

What advice would you give to someone thinking about opening or expanding a child care center?

First and foremost, when getting into any business it is imperative you run demographic reports, create conservative income vs expense reports, investigate other centers in the area and do as much research as possible. Intricately analyze all data to make sure that the child care center and or expansion thereof can be a profitable business.

Secondly, make sure that the area will support the product and or service model that you would like to provide.

Third, become part of a resource, training and support group such as Kris Murray's Child Care Success Academy. Doing so you learn from successful child care owners that have been in the business for endless years, with endless knowledge and experiences, that that can help you do the same.

Thoughts from Jennifer:

The sky's the limit.

CHILD CARE PROFILE

Kym Pomares

Courthouse Academy

Location: Virginia
Year Opened: 1992
# of Employees: 61
# of Locations: 1
2017 Gross Revenue: $1,880,000

How did you finance your first location?

I rented church space for a number of years. I financed the school with about $500.00 of my own money. (I started with ten 2-year-olds, one 3-year-old, and twelve 4-year-olds.) I was relatively content to stay in the church, but one day I was looking at the church bulletin board in the hallway and saw their notice that they were opening their own school the next year. That was how I found out I was being kicked out. I had nine months to relocate. I found land and a builder and then it proceeded to rain for four out of the nine months! Amazingly we made it by the move date! In order to build my location, I got a conventional loan and an SBA loan. The original building was over a million dollars and later I doubled the size of the building, spending another million.

What was the biggest mistake you made in your business in the first two years?

My biggest mistake was having the wrong business partner. After a couple of years, we went our separate ways, which was very difficult. We had opened three schools in three churches within two years. All were immediately profitable and grew rapidly. The downside of having such success so quickly is that I was making a lot of money without understanding what was working and what wasn't. So, when I started losing money, I didn't know what was wrong or how to correct it. I nearly went bankrupt.

What was the smartest business decision you have ever made?

Involving myself with Kris Murray's Child Care Success Academy and other successful business owners. The knowledge and support of these people have done so much to turn my business around.

What advice would you give to someone thinking about opening or expanding a child care center?

Know your numbers. Develop a dashboard with your key metrics so that you understand where you are making your money, where it is going, and what you should be charging.

Thoughts from Kym:

While this is not my quote, it is attributed to Winston Churchill, I find it to be so true. "Success is never certain, failure is never final." During rough periods I have repeated it to myself over and over again to help carry me through.

Chapter 3
The Financial Picture

This next chapter deals with the one area that I believe child care center owners drop the ball on the most, finances. The majority of owners who read this book do not know how to read a profit and loss statement, are unclear what a balance sheet is, and have had to borrow money at some point to make payroll.

If this is you, you are not alone. More than likely you are an educator who did not have any formal business education or training. The good news is your competitors are in the same boat as you are. With a little education you will be able to put your center in a much better financial position and be in great shape to expand should you wish to.

Before you begin reading the nuggets in this chapter I would like you to figure out your net worth. List all of your assets by what the approximate fair market value is (cash, property value, investments, automobiles, etc). Now list all of your liabilities (all debts including mortgage balances, auto balances, credit card balances, business or personal loan balances).

Now subtract liabilities from assets and you have your net worth. This should be a positive number, but for most people today it is a negative number. Knowing your starting point is the key to getting a plan for increasing your net worth.

When I started my first child care center I had a seriously negative net worth, but through hard work and dedication to a strict financial plan I had a $1 million-dollar net worth by the time I was in my early 40s and it has grown way past that point since. I do not tell you this to brag in any way, I want you to know what is possible with strong financial discipline and hard work. My goal was to retire at 50, and I could have if I had not met Kris Murray. I am so passionate about making a difference in the lives of others that when I got the opportunity to join her team, I put retirement on hold.

NUGGET #13:
Hire a Good CPA (Not an Accountant)

It seems that today everyone is a tax expert. With the invention of online tax software programs more and more people think they can do their own taxes.

The American tax code is thousands of pages thick, and making a mistake while doing your taxes could land you in jail. Never trust a million-dollar child care business to anyone other than a good, competent certified public accountant.

A CPA is licensed by a governing body of a state and has to pass certain educational and continuing educational requirements. Their name will also be on your tax document, so the IRS will know who prepared the document. This is important.

I pay a retainer fee to my CPA so that I can call him whenever I have a question throughout the year. I do not like to wait until taxes are due to ask tax related questions.

I also spend 2-3 hours with him in December of each year making sure that I am taking advantage of all possible deductions prior to the end of my fiscal year. Have your CPA review income, expenses and potential deductions for next year to see if there are any expenses you can bring forward or if there is income you may be able to defer into the following year. You must do this is before the fiscal year is over.

Each time I expanded my business to a new location, I would have my CPA run the numbers with me. He would share with me the tax ramifications of all aspects of the purchase and advise me on how to structure the lease or the purchase.

Your CPA needs to be someone that you can get on the phone on short notice, someone you can trust with your finances, and someone who wants to make sure you only pay the legal minimum in taxes.

NUGGET #14:
Know How to Read a Financial Statement

If you are the CEO of your child care business you should know how to read a financial statement.

One of the biggest causes of child care failures around the world is finances. Actually, it is not finances; it is lack of knowledge about finances.

Education is important, because if you do not understand the financial health of your business, your business will be in trouble and will never be able to successfully grow.

It is time to take some basic accounting classes, buy some books, and educate yourself.

There are several books on the market on understanding financial statements. At a minimum you will need to know how to read a balance sheet, a profit and loss statement, and as your business expands your banker will often ask you for a personal financial statement.

Your business checkbook is far different than your home checkbook. With your personal finances, when there is money in your account that is generally the money that's left after you pay your bills.

It is not the same with your business checkbook, hence where child care owners get into trouble. When a parent pays you a tuition payment that money is not yours to spend as you see fit. It does not work that way. You have to be able to manage your cash flow; failure to properly manage it will result in sure business failure. Educate yourself and you will be much better off.

I highly recommend reading these three books, all written by Robert Kiyosaki: *Cashflow Quadrant, Real Estate Riches, and Rich Dad, Poor Dad.* These books are responsible for laying the financial foundation in my business and in my personal life.

NUGGET #15:
Live Below Your Means

The key to surviving a financial downturn is living below your means during good times. At the time of publishing this book, things are good in America and most of the world as far as the unemployment rate, which is normally the leading indicator of child care business health.

What goes up, must eventually come down. Recessions normally happen every 10-15 years on average, having that knowledge will put you in a powerful position when it does happen, providing you are prepared.

If you are the owner of a successful child care center and are spending in your personal life 100% of the net profits from your business, you will more than likely be in trouble during an economic downturn.

As your business makes more and more money, do not increase your lifestyle to match the extra money until you have savings equal to at least 6 months' worth of operating expenses of your business (basically 50% of your annual gross revenue).

Once you have that money put away and invested, then you can increase your lifestyle as extravagantly as you wish, knowing that if tragedy or the economy drops enrollment by 35%, you have the means to stay afloat.

Living below your means is also a good idea to show your employees how humble you are. Driving around in a $100,000 car while paying your staff very little is never a good idea. You will never have someone work extra hard for you if they think you are making millions on the backs of their blood, sweat and tears. Be smart about what your employees see of your lifestyle.

NUGGET #16:
Every Two Years Look for a Better Deal

Every two years you are going to want to send things out to bid to always make sure you are getting the best deal.

Make a list of all of the service providers that you contract with for services. If you do some checking around, you might be able to find the same service for a better price. Examples include: lawn care, plumbing, electrical, fuel delivery, plowing, water delivery, coffee service, insurance, (car, liability, plumbing, workers compensation, healthcare, student accident, general practice).

Sixty days before a contract renews, contact each person who is in charge of the contract and let them know you are going out to bid for the contract and you wish them to submit a bid.

Contact three other service providers and have each one bid for the service you wish to contract for. You will have two choices when you receive a lower bid. You can accept the bid and change companies, or you can contact the current company and see if they will match the lowest bid (only do this if you are happy with the current company's service).

I have saved myself tens of thousands of dollars by doing this, and it keeps my vendor's honest. By them knowing I am doing this, they keep their annual increases to a minimum and keep costs competitive.

I also try to do business with people who do business with me. Survey your parents to see if any of them own a business where you can possibly barter child care for the service they offer, such as lawn mowing or cleaning services. Keep in mind that bartering is taxable under IRS rules.

NUGGET #17:
Have Saving Sub Accounts

I talk to clients all of the time, some who have $1 million in annual revenue, who have zero in savings. They are risking their entire business, and the livelihoods of everyone employed by them, because of poor financial choices.

How much should you save? My answer is simple, every penny you do not have to spend.

Most banks will allow you so to set up sub accounts under your main account. I have six of these under business and personal checking and savings accounts.

Some examples of what I use them for: vacation saving, quarterly and annual taxes, maintenance, renovations, expansion, and emergencies.

I set a fixed amount each month to be automatically transferred from my various accounts to all of these six accounts, and it is done without me even knowing it is being done. Out of sight, out of mind. By having a disciplined savings account program, I am able to have cash on hand when I want to take a vacation, buy a new company vehicle, make major renovations to one of my buildings, or the big enchilada; buying a new location, like I have done three times simply by writing a check.

I have been doing this for over ten years, and by being disciplined, I estimate I have saved tens of thousands of dollars in interest from borrowing I would have done to finance projects I have written a check for.

Having these growing sub accounts does another good thing; it strengthens your balance sheet. Having a healthy savings looks great to a bank when you do need to go fund a building purchase, or maybe a fleet of busses. It tells the banker you are a good credit risk because you are disciplined with your money.

NUGGET #18:
Your Center is Full of Used Equipment

Of all of the nuggets in this book, this is probably the one that I will get the most hate mail on.

Your center is full of used equipment. I am sorry, but once a snot nosed kid wipes a booger on your fancy expensive piece of child care furniture, it is now a used piece of equipment.

You clean up and sanitize that equipment and then the next day you still think it is good enough to be in your program. Why not go out and buy a new one each time a kid drools or sneezes on a toy?

My point is your center is full of used equipment which you think is good enough for the kids in your care. If I were to come in to your center and buy a piece of your furniture from you that you think is still good, and put it in my center, would it not be good enough for my kids? The answer is yes, it would!

Many of you reading this book are home providers and you want to open a center. My point here is you do not have to go out and spend a fortune furnishing your center with all of the latest and greatest expensive toys, look for used toys that centers, and home providers are selling.

Centers are going out of business all of the time, and I make a habit of searching these people out and going in and buying it all. I have bought tractor-trailer loads of child care equipment before. I have bought a lot off of Facebook Marketplace and Craigslist. I also have a contact at our local child care agency who gives me a heads up when she hears of a center closing (I want their equipment, their staff, their kids and possibly their building!). Put feelers out that you are always looking, so others will look for you. Be willing to travel a few hundred miles to buy a center full of equipment for your next location.

I have a storage unit and as I acquire good deals, I fill up my storage unit. When I need a new changing table, I first head to my storage unit to see what I have before buying a new one.

Since most of the equipment I have purchased at less than 20 cents on the dollar,

I estimate I have probably saved $200,000 or more in furnishing the nine centers I have opened.

Don't be afraid to buy a piece of used equipment, after all your center is full of used equipment that you think is good enough for the kids in your care!

NUGGET #19:
Have an Exit Strategy

We all get into child care because we want to help children, but there comes a time when we start thinking of an exit strategy.

For me that time came about six years ago. I had been in the child care business for over 14 years at that point, and I had thought I had done well for myself. The only problem was I had no equity because I didn't own any of my buildings.

I set a goal for purchasing real estate and to start acquiring centers with property I could purchase. Over the next three years I ended up buying seven properties, three of which I run child care centers out of; all without ever stepping foot in a bank (no I did not pay cash if that is what you were wondering).

I approached all of my landlords and they took me seriously when I made an offer. I am a model tenant. I fix a lot of my own maintenance issues, and I actually raised my own rent $150 a month because my landlord had not raised it in 5 years and I thought he deserved a raise. How is that for a good tenant!

One of my favorite sayings is *"chance favors the bold."* I made an offer to my landlord at one of my locations to purchase the building; he was so impressed with me that he offered to owner finance 100% of the deal. Since then I have bought four other properties from him, and he also financed a building we put a center in.

My exit plan early on was to sell the business and live on the rental income, but when my children started showing an interest in the business that changed. When my daughter Angel changed her major to early childhood education, I had a new, better plan.

Two years ago, when my daughter Brandy expressed interest in the business we started the transition of slowly transferring ownership over the next few years to both of them, so my wife Carol and I can retire. For us, the rentals will generate a very comfortable living for us until we start pushing up daisies.

If your exit strategy involves selling your business, be sure to hire a good business broker. It is best to sell a school that has been 85% full or better for the last 2-3 years. Contact your CPA and let them know you may want to sell in a few years, and he/she will help you get your financial house in order to make sure that you are in a good position to sell.

When is the best time to sell? When unemployment in your area is under 4% and you are 85% full or better, preferably 90% or better. If you sell when unemployment is higher, you will be commanding a much lower price. Buy low and sell high, that is the secret here!

Another tip is to reduce as much debt as you can to prop up your balance sheet and make the company more attractive, and to put more money in your pocket at the sale.

There are pros and cons to selling to a family member. The pros are you trust them and can give them credit that maybe a bank would not. The cons are you trust them and can give them credit that maybe a bank would not. Wait, did he just repeat himself? Yes. What are you going to do if a family member misses a required rent or installment payment? Will you foreclose or sue them? I have heard some horror stories from clients that were in business with family members that ended very badly. Be careful here is all I am saying.

If you do sell to a family member, make sure that person has worked at every position in the company for 2-3 years before purchasing the center for the same wage as other teachers doing the same job. They will then appreciate the sacrifice employees' make, and they will know what to expect when times are tough. Plus, this will show their level of commitment. My daughters have done every job in my company for many years and worked for minimum wage, I gave no special treatment just because they were my children. By doing this, they are highly respected by the staff as they take over ownership, even at a young age.

As you put together your exit plan, if it simply involves selling your business you are missing the boat. Owning as much real estate as possible and having good positive cash flow are the secrets to having an exit strategy that will be lucrative and long lasting.

NUGGET #20:
Have Written Financial Goals

When was the last time you sat down with a piece of paper and wrote down your financial goals? If you are like most people, the answer would probably be never.

In Nugget #1 I asked you to set some business goals. This is where I want you to start thinking of personal goals.

It is time to sit down and begin thinking about where you wish to be financially 5, 10 and 20 years from now. Put this book down and get a piece of paper and a pen and start writing down some goals.

- How much annually do I want 5, 10 and 20 years from now? $_____

- How much will my net worth be in 5, 10 and 20 years? $_____

- I will own $_____ worth of real estate in 5, 10 and 20 years?

- How much will I have saved in my retirement account in 5, 10 and 20 years? $_____

You will never reach a goal you do not set. By actually writing your goals down, and posting them on a goal board, you will tell your brain to go to work to make it happen.

What is a goal board? A goal board is something you hang on your wall that has your goals and dreams on it. If going to Hawaii is a goal of yours, place pictures of Hawaii on your goal board. If having a brand-new BMW is a goal of yours, get a picture of it and put it on your goal board. You will also want to write your written goals on the board as well.

By having a goal board, your brain gets to visually see the goals you are shooting for and will subliminally go to work to help you achieve them. This is fun to do, so make it a family affair. Have your children put their goals on the board as well and you will be teaching them a valuable lesson. Hard work pays off and dreams do come true.

NUGGET #21:
Make Part Time Care Profitable

I have coached hundreds of clients over the years and many of them were breaking even or even losing money on part-time children.

I get it. When you are first starting out, you will take whatever you can get and will pretty much accommodate any schedule a parent gives you. As you grow and get closer and closer to being full, part-time care can cost you dearly in two different ways.

The first way part-time will hurt you is it can limit full-time availability. If you have one day a week that is popular for part-time children, and the classroom fills that one day a week, you now cannot accept a new full-time child in that classroom.

The second way this costs you money is in overstaffing costs. When part-time care is not managed properly, and there are ups and downs in your staffing needs, you end up paying a lot more for staffing than necessary.

To make part-time profitable you need to surcharge it and manage it. What does it mean to surcharge part-time? If you are charging $200 a week for full-time care, what would you normally charge for someone that uses 50% of a full-time spot? Most centers charge 50%, and that is wrong! You need be charging at least a 15-20% premium on part-time spots to make up for the holes in the schedule it will create when you cannot offset part-time children.

I have experimented with many part-time variations over the last 20 years and have found one that has been extremely profitable for my company. We consider full-time care to be when a child attends over 30 hours a week. For part-time, we use hours attended instead of days attended. A child can attend 20-29.9 hours and pay 85% of the full-time rate. Let's say full-time is $200, part-time would be $170. I put the parent on a set schedule and I look for ways to offset part-time against each other. If you can get two $170 parents to share a $200 full time spot, YOU WIN BIG TIME!

Part-time management takes some work, but it is a way to oversell center capacity and make a much higher profit margin. Part-time flexibility also gives you a huge competitive advantage over your competitors who may be locking parents into a M/W/F or Tu/Thu type schedule, which is not very working parent friendly. I have seen some clients do this type of part-time schedule successfully, but most end up with much more demand for one or the other.

Be sure to build a spreadsheet and map out when all children will be attending each day to help identify holes in your schedule. Fill these holes with part-time and drop in children to help increase profitability. Full classrooms are much more profitable!

NUGGET #22:
Have a Scholarship Program

In the last 20 years I estimate I have given over $1 million dollars in scholarships away to needy families in my area.

We all hear sob stories of parents that are struggling, the best way to handle it is to have a scholarship program at your center that is managed by you.

You will only use your own money, as accepting donations from others will subject you to strict state and federal fundraising laws.

We let parents know when they tour we have a scholarship program at our center for families that may be struggling, and we ask them if they would like to apply when they tour.

We have them fill out an application, which will list their income and the reason they are seeking assistance. We match the income with the state and federal child care assistance minimums to first see if the parent would qualify for a state subsidy, which in many cases they do without even realizing it.

Our scholarships vary from waiving a registration fee to having part of their weekly copay forgiven. At no time do we ever give 100% scholarship. We also ask each parent that receives help from us to be sure at some point in their life to pay it forward and help someone else.

Set a budget each year for how much you would like to give and stick to that budget. Each time you give a reduced tuition or offer someone two weeks free to attend your center, use scholarship money. When a parent leaves me with a small balance, instead of sending them to collections I will always use scholarship money to pay off the debt.

You can also use scholarship money to write off the difference between what the state pays you and what the actual tuition at your center is if you do not charge the parent the full difference.

Feel free to use the fact that you have a scholarship program in your marketing materials and be as generous as your heart desires.

At no time can you collect money from parents to add to your scholarship program because then it would become a charity and would have to be registered at the state and federal level. Only use your own money and there will be no paperwork or filing requirements.

NUGGET #23:
Use Fees to Increase Revenue

The last time you booked a hotel on a travel site, they listed the price of the hotel, but they never list in bold print the additional fees that will be added. Resort fees have creeped into just about every hotel booking and are accepted as normal.

When a parent calls for your rates, and calls your competitor, they normally just ask you for your bottom line full-time rate.

Just about all centers charge a registration fee, and yours needs to be charged each time a parent registers, or re-registers. Some centers require parents to re-register annually.

Other fees include late payment fees, late pickup fees, annual supply fees, technology fees, a summer activities fee, a security fee, a maintenance fee, field trip fees, uniform fees, etc.

Be careful not to "fee" your parents to death, because they will get upset and might leave you over this. Providing a detailed explanation each time you require a fee will allow them to better understand why you are charging it. When they know why, it is easier for them to accept.

You can also consider having fundraisers to raise money in place of fees, or to reduce fees. You tell parents you need to raise $1,000 or get enough donations of school supplies to avoid all parents having to pay a supplies fee. By throwing the responsibility back to them, they cannot complain too much if no one helps and then everyone has to pay a shared supplies fee. Check with your state to ensure that you are legally allowed to hold a fundraiser.

NUGGET #24:
Invest in Your Business

The old adage goes *"It takes money to make money."* Outside of the Publisher's Clearing House Sweepstakes, I do not know of a way to make money without having first investing some money.

When you invest in the stock market, returns of 10% a year would be considered as excellent by most people. When it comes to marketing, you are looking for much higher yields for your investment into your marketing budget.

Of the hundreds of clients, I have helped over the years, very few of them had a marketing budget before they met me. They were struggling in all areas of their business from enrollment to finances to staffing and having to do it all alone without any help.

The child care millionaire spends 3-5% or more of gross revenues on marketing, advertising and professional development. I know of some clients that spend close to 10% in this area. As long as you are getting a good ROI, why not invest more here?

In 2015 when I met Kris Murray for the first time, I had a very small marketing budget. The truth is I was in business for over 17 years at that point and thought I knew everything about marketing and advertising. I was wrong!

When I hired Kris Murray as my coach in 2015 she taught me that in order to grow your business, you must first invest in your business. This changed the way I looked at everything. The results were phenomenal. For every dollar I spent in coaching and personal development through my marketing budget, I received $20 back in return. Imagine putting $100 in the stock market and a year later you had $2000!

Obviously, you have to actually have a budget to create a marketing budget, so if you do not have one now is the time to create one. If you do not have a budget, you are in the vast majority of child care owners. This is one area you do not want to be in the majority. Step out, create a budget, and allocate money for marketing. You will be so glad you did!

NUGGET #25:
Have a Will and a Living Will

When you have some time, buy a newspaper and open up to the obituary section. Everyone on the page more than likely thought they had one more day. Unless suicide is involved, we don't know when our last day will be.

People your age die each and every day. Lots of them! Why would you ever want to leave a mess for your loved ones to have to clean up?

I have seen families destroyed fighting over scraps of inheritance from someone who did not leave clear wishes as to what happens when that final day comes.

The child care millionaire has thought of every possible scenario and has a last will and testament, and a living will (sometimes called an advanced healthcare directive).

A will allows your heirs to clearly know what your intentions are upon your demise. You can dictate the way you want your business run, have your money allocated per your wishes, and the most important part; your is business protected.

Your employees and parents deserve continuity should your last day come. What would your child care families do if you were not around to run the company? Would your employees be able to get paid should you not be around? Would everything fall apart?

What if you are on life support? Who would make business decisions? Who would approve payroll? Who would run the company? Who would have power of attorney over your affairs?

Make sure someone in your family knows where your will is kept and have an executor you can trust to quickly ensure things are done according to your wishes. This person will need to make sure rent, utilities, and employees are paid on time; so the business can run uninterrupted.

I do not apologize for making you think about the inevitable; we will all die. Some of us will die sooner than others. Other people should not have to suffer due to your lack of planning. Call an attorney and create your will and living will right away. I can promise you will sleep better at night, and if you do die in your sleep, your business will be protected.

NUGGET #26:
Don't Step Over Dollars to Pick Up Pennies

As a business owner you need to ensure that every dollar you spend makes you more dollars. You also want to make sure that every hour you spend gives you more hours. Let me explain what I mean.

Time is money, and money is time. Being so tight with your money that you do not let it work for you will have the adverse effect on your life and in your business.

There are not many child care millionaires that have not hired an assistant to help them with the day to day in their business. The ones who have not would more than likely be more successful today if they had done so earlier.

Each time you do a task that can be delegated for a certain hourly rate, you are now working for that hourly rate. For example. If you are an owner and you are driving the school bus each morning, and you could hire someone for $10 an hour to do the same thing, you are now working for $10 an hour.

The $10 you save from not having a bus driver is money saved, but it is not money earned; it is actually a loss. As a business owner you need to be free to be able to spend your time on high payoff activities of your business, where one hour of your time yields hundreds of dollars in revenue to the company.

If you were to take that same hour you were driving the bus and create a flyer that you distributed to a local business, and enrolled 2 children from that flyer, that one hour made you tens of thousands of dollars.

The same theory holds true for marketing dollars. You could hold onto that extra thousand dollars, but putting it to work could yield you tens of thousands of dollars to your company when you gain enrollments from your marketing efforts.

Don't step over dollars to pick up pennies. Delegate and be smart with your time. You may think you cannot afford to let go, trust me you can't afford not to!

NUGGET #27:
Manage Your Cash Flow

If I can point to one area where child care center owners fail the most often, it is cash flow management.

Learning to manage cash flow properly is the single most important thing you can learn for the long-term financial health of your business.

Why do most business owners fail? It is simple. They treat their business checkbook like their personal checkbook. If you have money in your personal checkbook, normally that money can be spent how you wish. That philosophy does not work in a business.

I have clients tell me all of the time they feel that have no money left at the end of each month, or worse, they have to borrow money just to make payroll. If you have had to borrow money to make payroll in the last 12 months, you have a cash flow problem that needs to be addressed.

In your business checkbook, very little of that money is personally yours. What do I mean? You are constantly creating liabilities in your company. Each payday, you are creating tax liabilities. Some of the money that you collect belongs to the IRS and your state revenue agency. You may also collect money from employees that you have to pay a health insurer or a retirement account administrator. You are charging things on your credit card that have to be paid at some point in the future.

The bottom line is you have to get good at knowing how much of what is in your checkbook is actually yours, and what belongs to others. A simple way to do it when your business is small is to have a checkbook line item called unpaid liabilities, and have it set for a future date, so it appears at the bottom of your electronic checkbook.

On this liability line include all of your liabilities, including your monthly credit card debt that has been charged but remains unpaid. This will help to give you a clearer picture of what your actual "spendable" cash is, and what is allocated for future spending.

I recommend paying a small salary to yourself that you can live on, and do not take anything else out of the business for 6 to 12 months. Let the profits accumulate in the business and take them quarterly at minimum, and make sure that you have a strict savings regimen as I recommend in Nugget #17. By letting profits accumulate you start getting a sense for how much cash flow you need to float all of your liabilities each month. Don't worry, as long as you only buy things you need, the profit will all be yours when you are ready to have it distributed to you.

I would recommend sitting down with your CPA to discuss ways for you to manage cash flow better. This is one area that if you get wrong, it is going to put you out of business in a hurry.

NUGGET #28:
Have a Strict Annual Budget

I have clients who ask me all the time how to create an annual budget. What I always tell them is to start from last year's numbers. Have your CPA give you an excel spreadsheet of last year's income and expenses, figure out your projected income for the year, then estimate what your expenses will be for every line item.

While I have a CPA that I trust, I know all money in and out of my business. I analyze numbers monthly and make sure that my spending and revenue numbers are on track. I also have a very strict savings regimen. Following a strict budget will strengthen your business significantly, make it more valuable should you wish to sell someday, and give you reserves should there be an economic downturn.

I recommend buying a book on budgeting and finances and read it. The more educated you are, they more likelihood you will achieve financial success in your business.

If you discipline yourself with a strict budget and learn the secrets to good cash flow management, your net business revenue will grow, and your stress level will shrink!

NUGGET #29:
Never Lie, Cheat or Steal

Integrity is the one of those things that is crucial to have to be successful in business. It is also something that can be lost in an instant.

When I started my first business I had a poster hung on my wall and it had some success principles on it. One that had always stuck with me the rest of my life was *"Never lie, cheat or steal and always strike a fair deal."*

Honesty and integrity are things that are vital to have as a business owner. You need to be above board in every area of your life. Once integrity is lost, it is almost impossible to get back.

The easiest way to lose the respect of your employees is to make a mistake on their paycheck. If you make too many errors your staff will feel like you are cheating them. This is one area you have to be right 100% of the time. If an employee feels that you stiffed them on a paycheck, or in their paid time off, they will never trust you again.

Your parent-clients will need to trust you as well. If your business finances are a mess, chances are you will make mistakes on parent payments and can cause real strife. Sometimes a parent will leave and never tell you the real reason they left, and it may be because they felt like they were lied to or cheated in some way.

Always be sure to be totally honest and fair in all of your dealings, and make sure that communication lines are always open. If you promise someone something, be sure to follow through and put these words on the wall in your office: "Never Lie, Cheat or Steal and Always Strike a Fair Deal."

NUGGET #30:
Smart Debt Only

Debt is not your enemy, but it can be. Using money to leverage more money is smart for business growth, but you have to make sure that you accumulate smart, manageable debt.

There are a lot of financial books that tell you that you should be as leveraged as possible, borrowing huge gobs of money and having it make money for you. There is some truth to this, but only if you are a smart money manager and you are not averse to risk taking.

I have opened 9 centers, own millions of dollars in investment properties, and I have never borrowed a penny from a bank to do so. There is nothing wrong with borrowing from a bank, but the rules are much more strict when dealing with a bank than with dealing with other forms of private financing.

You will need to borrow at various times as you grow your business. Some borrow at initial startup, some to finance expansion, others to buy equipment. Whatever the reason, you need to make sure you are comfortable with the terms of the arrangement, and how it affects the ability to obtain financing in the future.

The smartest debt is low interest, tax deductible debt. If you are financing a small amount, a home equity line of credit from your bank is probably the best way to go. I recommend that all child care business owners have the maximum amount possible available to them in the form of a home equity line of credit to use to grow your business. This money is never to be used for anything that does not increase revenue substantially. It is never used to pay payroll, buy supplies, or increase your personal lifestyle. Instead it should be used for adding licensing capacity, purchasing another location or paying down high interest credit card debt that is disrupting business cash flow.

When you made your 2, 5 and 10-year goals did you list anything about being debt free? That is the ultimate long- term objective.

Keep in mind when you borrow commercially, many of the loans will balloon in a few years. This is debt that should be aggressively paid down. By doing so it will put you in a much better place financially.

NUGGET #31:
Pay Down Debt...Smartly

Paying down personal and business debt should be part of an overall success strategy for your business. This needs to be a priority for all businesses.

I prefer the aggressive, results driven approach to debt elimination. It starts with making a spreadsheet of all of your credit card debt first and sorting it by the highest interest debt first. Then list any non-collateralized loans. Next list all collateralized loans. Lastly list all tax-deductible debt such as home or business loans, and home equity loans.

When you have made the decision that you will not get into any more debt, it is time to cut up all of the credit cards, except the one with the lowest interest rate that we will be paying down last.

Why do I want you to cut up the cards? Because as you pay them off you are going to be tempted to start using them again, you will not be able to help yourself. You have to cut the card, pay it off, and close the account. There is no other way to solve this problem.

You will need to figure how much you can afford each month extra to apply to your principal each month. After you have read this entire book you will have found ways to save money in your business. Use what you have learned to take that money and put all of the extra each month on the highest interest credit card first. Do this each and every month until that one card is paid off.

Once a card is paid off it is very important to call the credit card company and close the account. If you don't, you will be tempted to spend again, and you simply cannot afford to go backwards.

Continue doing this month after month until all of your credit cards are paid off, and then vow to never pay interest on a credit card again. I love using my credit cards for business, it is an amazing cash flow weapon that I have, but I pay my balance off each month and have never paid interest. Debt is fine, providing it is smart debt. Paying 15-20% interest on a credit card is great for the credit card company, but horrible for the consumer. The time to make a change is now. Make a decision and then make a plan. Make a plan then put it into action. Before you know it, you will be debt free!

NUGGET #32:
Never Pay Credit Card Interest

Credit can help make you rich, but it can also put you in the poorhouse.

I made a decision about 12 years ago that I would screw the credit card companies instead of the other way around. So far, my plan has worked flawlessly. In the last 12 years I have charged millions of dollars on credit cards and have not paid a penny in interest.

Not only have I not paid any interest, they have paid me to use their cards; and they have paid me handsomely! My secret? Reward credit cards.

Since my wife and I like to travel, and the cost of airline travel is not cheap, we decided we would get an Airline Credit Card. We started with a U.S. Air Mastercard®, which later became American Airlines Mastercard®.

I got a card for business use and I got another one for personal use. I charge everything I possibly can on my cards, earning miles I can later exchange for flights around the world. Since I own a business that spends hundreds of thousands of dollars each year, I can charge items such as: food, supplies, equipment, technology, telephone, internet, insurance, oil, natural gas, fire system, sprinkler system, office supplies, and a whole lot more.

It is all stuff I would have to write a check for anyway, so they are actually paying me to use their money! I have my account on auto pay and it pays my statement balance entirely off on the due date each and every month. This means I pay zero interest!

Over the years my wife and I have flown first class to the Caribbean dozens of times, and never paid a penny for our flights. We flew my family and parents to Hawaii one year, and it cost us nothing for airfare. I estimate I have received over $50,000 in free airline tickets over the years.

Whether you want to get an airline card or maybe a Discover Card® that pays you cash back, get something that gives you cash or the equivalent of cash for using the card, but never pay interest. Doing so would negate all of the benefits of card membership.

NUGGET #33:
Frugality is Key

The child care millionaire is frugal and loves a good deal. Whenever you need to have work done, be sure to get estimates from 2-3 reputable vendors to make sure you are getting a good price.

When purchasing a vehicle, never buy a new one. Driving off the lot kisses 50% of your equity away. Purchasing a 2- 3 year old vehicle is the best investment. You pay 50% of the cost of a new vehicle and it still has low miles.

When shopping for items that you purchase regularly always look around for the best possible deal. If you allow your team to order things, expect them to always find the best deal. When you find a really good deal on something you purchase regularly, be sure to buy in bulk and store it for later use.

There is nothing wrong with being frugal in your business, especially when you are just starting out. Even today, I am always looking for the best possible deal in everything that I do. I hate throwing my hard-earned money away.

NUGGET #34:
Credit Cards vs. ACH

I am going to sound like a bit of a hypocrite here. I do not like child care centers accepting credit cards if you live in a state where you cannot pass credit card fees onto the customer.

Credit card fees are eating at the bottom line at centers around the world. I have some clients paying $30,000 a year in credit card fees, this is ridiculous!

I live in a state where I would have to eat these fees, and that is something I am not prepared to do. The only way I will accept a credit card is when a parent is behind on payment and there is no other way they are able to pay. Be sure to check your state law before trying to pass on this fee.

ACH on the other hand is a very smart option for parents. Normally fees are minimal, and the convenience is amazing. Find a company that will debit the parent and put the money in your account within two days for optimum cash flow management.

If your state allows you to pass on credit card fees to the consumer, and you charge them 100% of the fee you are charged, then I say go for it. Barring that, stick with ACH and you will be in much better financial shape at the end of the day.

CHILD CARE PROFILE

Andrea Wortman

Club K After School Zone

Location: Oregon
Year Opened: 2006
# of Employees: 60
# of Locations: 12
2017 Gross Revenue: $2,076,478

How did you finance your first location?

The first Club K location was financed from a $2500 loan from another child care center that I owned at the time. That center was financed from an SBA loan and partial owner financing.

What was the biggest mistake you made in your business in the first two years?

Learning to navigate and share space with others. Also, being too trusting of customers and staff.

What was the smartest business decision you have ever made?

Learning to cut my losses and move on whether it is with a parent we cannot please no matter what we do or it's a staff member who is not meeting our expectations.

What advice would you give to someone thinking about opening or expanding a child care center?

Don't be afraid to take that leap of faith, go in with your eyes open, do your due diligence beforehand, have cash reserves. There will be unplanned negative surprises, be prepared for them.

Thoughts from Andrea:

Watch every penny! Every penny counts!

CHILD CARE PROFILE

Amber Rogers

Palmetto Preschool & Learning Center, LLC.

Location: South Carolina
Year Opened: 2010
# of Employees: 35
# of Locations: 1 (plus 1 under construction)
2017 Gross Revenue: $1.4 million

How did you finance your first location?

We leased our first building from a church that had closed down their private school. We had an investor finance the building that we moved our first center to once we outgrew the building we were renting from the church. We paid cash for the land for building number two and are doing a conventional loan for the building.

What was the biggest mistake you made in your business in the first two years?

Allowing parents to carry balances and not holding firm to our policies for fear that we'd lose families.

What was the smartest business decision you have ever made?

Networking with child care providers outside of our local area and with other individuals outside of the child care industry.

What advice would you give to someone thinking about opening or expanding a child care center?

If your center is full or close to full, look at all of your options and figure out a way to make expansion a reality. Don't spend too long talking yourself out of it, instead focus your energy on what you need to do to make it happen.

Thoughts from Amber:

- *To be profitable you must remember you are running a business and not a charity, but that doesn't mean you can't still be charitable to those in need. Finding the optimal balance will bring you both mental peace and financial health.*

- *Teachers are the heartbeat of our centers, so we must make sure they know how much they are valued.*

- *Leadership and management are NOT the same thing; Make sure everyone in your organization understands and is living the difference.*

CHILD CARE PROFILE

Curt & Kathy Gray

Creative Critters Learning Centers

Location: Virginia
Year Opened: 2006
# of Employees: 35
# of Locations: 4
2017 Gross Revenue: $1.093 Million

How did you finance your first location?

Home equity loan in the amount of $50,000.

What was the biggest mistake you made in your business in the first two years?

I had no clue how to manage or lead my staff.

What was the smartest business decision you have ever made?

Continuing to expand even when I wanted to give up. Joining the Kris Murray Child Care Success Academy has helped me to work on my business and not in it.

What advice would you give to someone thinking about opening or expanding a child care center?

Have good financial people behind you to guide and lead you to make smart business decisions. Bigger is not always better. Start small and learn the business and develop yourself as a leader.

Thoughts from Kathy:

Anyone can manage someone. Leadership is an art that needs to be learned and comes from the heart.

Chapter 4
Operations

In this chapter I will give you nuggets on the operations side of your business that can help you be more profitable. Operations are the day to day things you do that are the foundation of your business.

I wish I could tell you I did all of these nuggets from day one of my business, if I did I would be lying. Many of them I learned along the way through trial and error and several of them I learned only in the last few years from my mentor and friend Kris Murray.

I caution you on trying to change too much in your business all at once. I recommend that you take 2-3 nuggets a month and try to implement them into your program until they are mastered then take on a couple more. Some will work amazingly well, and others will not work in your center because of many factors. Your goal is to find what works and do more of it and find out what is not working and either find a way to make it work or stop doing it.

NUGGET #35:
Have an Operations Manual

One of my fellow coaches, Jennifer Conner, turned me onto the importance of having a detailed operation manual.

The child care millionaire is detail oriented and must have systems in place to ensure that every possible scenario is covered so there is no guessing what to do in the absence of the owner.

You will never be able to get out of the overwhelm of your business (or ever be able to take extended vacations) without having systems in place that ensure that no matter what happens, there is a policy in place to deal with the situation.

An operations manual is a living, breathing document that will never be finished. It will be always evolving into something better and more detailed over time.

To manage multiple schools, it is imperative that all directors are on the same page on all policies, so an operations manual is what makes that happen.

To start creating one, open a shared document and start banging away at the keyboard as situations occur. Start with an outline and then you can start picking sub-categories.

An example would be the category of parent payments. You would want to break that down further by writing a policy for the following: accepting payments, late payments, ACH payments, credit card payments, bounced checks, checks not signed or dated, and non-payment.

Make sure you pick a software that gives you the ability to search. One program I like is Microsoft® OneNote®, it is very user friendly and completely searchable.

You will want to make the document readable by all, but editable only by you or your designee. That way the document you worked so hard on does not accidentally get erased or sabotaged by a deranged staff member.

As your business grows, and you get further and further removed from the day to day operations, the more you will have to have an operations manual guiding your team in all areas. It is not as good as having you there, but it is the next best thing. Consider your operations manual your Siri®, always there to help you or your team when you call on her.

NUGGET #36:
How to Work with a Spouse or Business Partner

Over the years I have coached dozens of husband and wife teams, as well as non-related business partners. There was one key factor in all of them that made them successful; they learned how to get along while working closely together.

I get asked all the time how I do it, how I can spend 24 hours a day, each and every day, working alongside my wife. My answer back to them is always the same, *"I couldn't imagine not spending 24 hours a day with the person I love more than anyone else in the whole world."*

Carol and I have been married 27 years and have worked together almost all of that time. We have mastered the art of working together and I will share some of our secrets.

We each have established lanes and we each have things in the business we are responsible for. In our business I handle all financial matters, Carol handles more of the day to day operations. I stay out of her way, and she stays out of mine. We meet at least weekly on things we need to have open discussion on, and we always figure it out if we have a disagreement.

When you do spend 24 hours a day with someone, it creates some boundary issues. What I mean is that since you are always together you feel the need to always be in business mode, and that can be dangerous.

You have to be able to separate the two. What Carol and I do is have a time each day when work stops and relaxing starts; our time is 7 p.m. It is at that point that we are not allowed to discuss anything work related, the cell phones get silenced, and we sit and hold hands and watch some television or read together. We have been doing this for many years, and it has brought us much closer together and made our business stronger.

Now if you have a business partner that is not a spouse or domestic partner, I would not recommend holding hands each night before bed, that would be weird. However, the same rules apply, there has to be a point each day where work stops for both of you and relaxing starts. Agree to set those ground rules and you will find a much happier partnership.

Be sure to have clear responsibilities written out that each partner is responsible for and try your best to always stay in your established lane. This will help to avoid conflict and will make your business a lot more productive instead of both partners doing the same tasks, which would not be a good use of time.

If you do not have a spouse or a business partner then you do not have to split the money with anyone!

NUGGET #37:
Don't Necessarily Follow a School Model

If you run a child care center, and do not have an elementary school attached to your center, I am writing this nugget just for you.

There is one sure fire way to gain market share in your community and steal clients from other centers; stop acting like a public school.

What do I mean? Do you close for the summer like a public school? Do you pay wages and benefits like a public school? Do parents get to attend your center free thanks to hard working taxpayers? More than likely you cannot answer yes to any of these.

If you are not a public school, why do you run your center like one? If you do, you are not alone. I have many competitors who have gone out of business using this model, which in my opinion is non-parent friendly.

A public school has no competition. Public schools are funded 100% from tax dollar collection. They can do whatever they want, and a parent cannot really do anything about it. They can close when there are snow flurries outside, they can take several weeks of the year off, and they can close for the summer.

Child care centers have competition; thus, the marketplace dictates the policies. Those that do not follow a school model are more parent friendly, which will result in many more children.

Whenever you inconvenience a working parent by closing too many days, he/

she will eventually look for a more convenient option. I have been operating for 20 years and have never shut down for a week for a school vacation, my parents would freak out. They would head very fast to my competitor down the road that does not inconvenience them.

If you live in the north, snow days are common. Kids have to ride school busses, which is why schools close. If you do not transport children, why are you closing when you get an inch of snow? Many parents still have to work, why would you inconvenience them? Only bring in staff members that want to commute in the weather and require parents to only use care if they have to work.

The more you make your center more convenient to your customers, the better chance you will have to capture market share and dominate your market. Be unique and specialize in convenience and you will reap the rewards.

NUGGET #38:
Consistency is the Key

Remember the story of the tortoise and the hare? Slow and steady wins the race.

In Nugget #3 I tell you about a book *The Slight Edge* by Jeff Olson, where you will learn the fine art of consistency. Since I know many of you will not order that book, I am going to tell you a little about one of the key tenants in the book and that is the power of consistency.

It takes 21 days to form a habit. Our brains put tasks we do into certain parts of the brain based on how often we need to utilize them. The more we do something, the more the brain familiarizes itself with the process and it can do it without active thought.

To give you an example; when you drove to work this morning did you remember opening your house door, walking outside, then closing it, walking to your car, unlocking the car door, opening the door, sitting down, closing the door, pulling the seat belt over your chest, clicking the seat belt, depressing the brake pedal, putting the key into the ignition, turning the ignition, putting it into drive, looking to see if the coast is clear, releasing the brake pedal, and pressing the gas pedal? Your brain did all of that in a few seconds and you do not remember doing any of it.

All of those actions were habits that were created by consistency. The first time you drove you had to teach your brain what the accepted procedure was, and once you had done it 21 days in a row, it became a habit.

The same holds true for our business. You need to develop consistent, daily habits that will help you to grow your business. What negative habits have you developed in your business? Do your parents pay late or have large balances? Do you let employees come in late each day and do not say anything?

As your business grows you can become overwhelmed if you do not develop consistent daily habits that you practice each and every day. Doing a little each day towards your goals will make them come true, I am living proof of that. I am exactly in life today where I predicted I would be four years ago. Why? I did a little bit each and every day and I let the power of *The Slight Edge* work in my life. It will work wonders for you!

NUGGET #39:
Work ON Your Business Instead of IN Your Business

The number one complaint I receive from clients is that they are overwhelmed. Why are they overwhelmed? There are normally two main reasons; they don't trust others, or they cannot afford to trust others.

Most child care millionaires are multi-site owners. Since we have not yet perfected the art of human cloning (I am anxiously awaiting this day, so I can clone my amazing wife!) we can only be in one place at a time. Which means most multi-site owners have learned the art of delegation. If they haven't, then they are twice as stressed as a single site owner. I can promise you, no one who has five schools has a problem with delegation.

If you want to work on your business, instead of in your business, you need to get out of your business. What do I mean? Work from home, get a corporate office, or work at Starbucks. Whatever it takes to get away from the distractions of the center. An hour away from your center is normally more productive than four hours in the center for most people.

If you have four or more schools I would recommend a corporate office away from your home and away from your schools. By doing this you can trust your schools to run without you, you can get more work done, and you can leave work at the end of the day and head home to a no work zone and relax.

If you are a single site owner, I know how busy you are. I worked harder when I had one location than I worked when having seven centers open. Why is that? I learned the art of duplication and delegation. I duplicated myself by delegating to competent staff that I could trust and empowered them to make decisions on my behalf.

One of the biggest failures of center owners is that they expect perfection from their directors and expect them to work as hard, if not harder than they do. This is simply not realistic.

I have a rule of thumb. If a director is great at enrollment, loves kids, treats the staff great, and is respected by her team, I can look past a lot of imperfections elsewhere. I know if I can get a director to have 85% of the commitment to my business, that is good enough for me. I will drive myself crazy trying to get all of my directors to 100%. It is not realistic.

The worst problems I have ever faced with clients that I coach are owners who have no background in child care when they buy a center and come in and start trying to run a child care like their corporate job. Regimented, systemized processes for everything. While processes are important, loving and caring for the children always has to be the number one priority over everything else.

Once you find a director that can perform at the 85% and above level, embrace it and start delegating so you can work on your business. You can coach them gently over time to get them in the 90%+ range, but you must be willing to be satisfied with 90%. I know I am!

As the owner, every hour you have to spend working in instead of on your business costs a lot of money. Why is that? When you are working on your business you are working to increase revenue. Working in your business normally does nothing to increase revenue, it actually costs you money and stresses you out!

NUGGET #40:
Hire a Coach

Tiger Woods has a coach. Tom Brady has a coach. Name me one professional athlete that does not have a coach, some have many coaches. Why? There is only so much you can do by yourself, a coach can see things in you that you do not see yourself. A coach will make you better.

As child care owners we sometimes get blinded by our business. We work in our business instead of on our business. We are so busy putting fires out each day that we do not have time to grow our business. We are exhausted and feel that we are just spinning our wheels. Have you ever had a day where you feel like you accomplished absolutely nothing? Do you have many of these?

The best example for what a coach does is this. Picture you are in a forest and there are trees everywhere. You can only see the trees in front of you, and nothing else. More than likely, this is where you are at currently in your business. You can't see the forest, you can only see the trees.

A coach will take you up to 10,000 feet and allow you to look down on your business so you can see the whole forest. Once we see the big picture, we can then put processes in place to give you the time to start working on your business instead of in your business.

Who needs a coach? Everyone. Whether you are a center owner of a small center, or you own 15 locations you need a coach!

Being a child care owner is just about the loneliest job in the world. Some days everyone is mad at you. Employees, parents, kids, even your dog. Having a coach gives you someone to pat you on the back, to bounce ideas off of, to work on goals with, and hold you accountable for those goals. The money you pay for a coach will come back to you multiplied.

When I hired Kris Murray in 2015 to be my coach, I had no idea she would help me increase my revenues by over $750,000 a year in less than two years. She was able to get me to think much differently about how I approached every facet of my business. She encouraged and inspired me to be the best I can be. When she asked me to join her team in 2017 to coach other struggling business owners, I was excited.

When you do hire a coach, make sure it is someone who has qualifications. Are they certified? Have they built a successful center or multiple centers? Have they accomplished things in their business that you have not? Do they have satisfied clients?

Let me help you change your life! If you are a child care center owner and you are struggling in any area of your business that you need coaching for, send me an email at brian@childcaremillionaire.com.

NUGGET #41:
Have an Emergency Plan of Action

Emergencies happen, this is simply a fact of life. I have a positive mindset, and always believe things are going to be okay but I am also a realist who knows that life happens.

Be prepared for any situation that can cause your program to be shut down either short or long term. This is the key to surviving long term in this business.

What would you do if a child died in your program today? Who would be your first call? Would you talk to the police? Would you speak to the press? What would you say to child care licensing? Should the employee who was watching the child be immediately fired? So many questions!

What would happen to your program if a natural or man-made disaster struck and your building was not functional for days, weeks or months? Earthquake, flooding, tornado, hurricane, sinkhole, blizzard, lightning, fire, vandalism, or terrorism. Anything can happen!

The best time to prepare for an emergency is before it happens. Here is a list of things to have lined up in case of a natural or man- made disaster.

1. Have a game plan to protect staff and children in the event of a natural disaster.

2. Have adequate insurance to protect you including loss of business income should your business become unusable. Make sure you have proper coverage amounts.

3. Have 2-3 days of emergency food, water, and first aid supplies on hand in case help can't get to you right away.

4. Make sure your parents know what your plan is in case you have to vacate your premises, so they would know where to find their child if phone lines are down.

5. Have an attorney on retainer to call anytime you have legal questions. When

anything happens in your program that can affect your license or your employee's livelihoods, your attorney is the first call.

- Talking to the police without a lawyer present is not wise if there is a criminal investigation. Also make sure you always have an attorney present during all questioning of staff during abuse or neglect allegations, where the reputation of the business is at stake.

6. Always go through your attorney when dealing with the press on any matters that can draw serious negative attention to your center.

7. Make sure you have employment practices liability insurance. This will protect you in case you are sued for discrimination of any kind.

8. Make sure you have wage and hour insurance protection as well, once again to protect the company.

9. If you have more than one location, and you have employees that travel between locations, be sure they are not doing so on company time. Have them clock in and out prior to travel and pay them mileage. Be sure to call your insurance provider and add non-owned auto rider to your policy. This will protect you in case of accident.

10. Make sure your operations manual has a detailed process which lists all possible scenarios and what has to happen with each. That way when you are frazzled during an emergency you just have to pull out a check list and read and follow.

11. Be sure to have a backup plan should your school be uninhabitable for weeks or months. It has happened to a few of my clients over the years. It is always good to think of a plan beforehand when you are thinking clearly.

I pray that something like this never happens to your business, but I do know, statistically speaking, many who are reading this nugget right now will face a situation I have previously described. My wish is that I have helped you better prepare.

NUGGET #42:
Use a Phone Script

Before I met Kris Murray I never in my wildest dreams ever thought to have my director use a phone script. They had been doing calls and tours for years, why would they need to read a script?

When I joined Kris Murray's coaching program in 2015, I blindly put into practice all of the things she told me would grow my program. One of those things was using a phone script.

Being excellent on the phone is one of the most important qualities of a good director. The director needs to be able to make a great first impression of the center: be polite, be empathetic, be a great listener, and be organized enough to capture the proper information.

The script needs to be worded in such a way that it seems like he/she is not reading at all. It needs to be practiced and role played until perfected.

Giving out rates is not a good idea on the initial call. Most people will want to start there, but a good director will quickly segue by immediately asking questions of the caller and will have the tour booked before the caller realizes that the rate question was never answered.

The purpose of a phone script is to capture the caller's name, email and cell number. Why is this important? You will want to continually market to this person, regardless if they enroll at your center or not.

A script helps the person who answers the call to get 100% capture of the most important things that are needed to collect on the call. It also ensures nothing gets forgotten and helps to save time by focusing on setting up the tour as the number one priority.

Answering too many questions allows the caller to have enough information on the phone to make a decision on whether or not to attend. You never want a caller to make a decision on enrollment until that person has toured. A phone script will help to increase the number of callers who convert to tours.

Important items to include on your script that you will want to capture during the call:

1. Name of caller, email and cell number
2. Child's name and age.
3. Days/times of care needed.
4. When they would need to start.
5. Be sure to create scarcity (Nugget #44).
6. What is the most important item they are looking for in a center?
7. How will they pay? (cash or state assistance?)
8. Book the tour, give them a choice between two times.

Using a script makes it easy to train how to answer the phone and it can be duplicated easily. If the person who answers the phone is out sick, anyone can answer the phone the same way.

Be sure to have the person who answers the phone write down all of the information he/she can remember and have it ready for the tour. When that person shows up for a tour, whatever they said on the initial call will be used to persuade them during the tour. Example: If the parent says that little Johnnie is allergic to eggs on the phone, be sure to repeat it back to the mom on the tour what your procedures are to ensure Johnnie does not get eggs. Listening intently on the phone call sets the stage for a tour that converts!

NUGGET #43:
Use a Tour Checklist

The child care millionaire has processes in place that are simple and easily duplicatable.

The average child care tour should be short (under 15 minutes) and should be an orchestrated event. It should be delivered by the team member with the highest level of sales and people skills.

I get pushback all of the time from clients when I use the term "selling" when referring to a tour. You are selling your center! You are trying to convince a person who does not know you to trust you to care for their most precious commodity on Earth for the sum of tens of thousands of lifetime customer dollars. This is selling, and the quicker an owner realizes this the quicker they will realize that the person doing the tour needs to be excellent in sales, and also trained in sales.

Invest in sales training techniques for any staff member who will be giving a tour. There are many books and courses you can purchase that will help someone gain the sales skills necessary to sell a $50,000+ child care product (lifetime customer value).

An airline pilot who has flown 10,000 hours still has to use a checklist for everything they do before, during and after a flight. Why? To ensure that nothing gets forgotten. A tour is the same way. A checklist will allow you to do the same tour each and every time and will ensure that nothing is forgotten.

Having a tour checklist makes the process easily duplicatable for anyone that you would like to teach the process to. Have them follow the checklist each and every time and doing a tour does not seem so hard. Couple this with some sales training that will help with the close and you will see tour conversion rates upwards of 50% or higher.

It is up to you what you put on the tour checklist. What I would recommend are things to make sure all of the five senses are covered. Things that can be easily forgotten should be added to the list. Items such as:

Pre-Tour:
1. How does the center smell?
2. Did you look outside for any trash?
3. Light music playing in background?
4. Did you notify all teachers a tour is coming in?
5. Place a welcome sign on the front door with their name on it.
6. Send email and text reminders of tour to your prospect.

Tour (15-20 minutes tops):
7. Did you offer them a snack or a beverage?
8. Discuss whatever hot button issues they discussed with you on initial call.
9. Have a tour stop in your entranceway that highlights your teachers, your

core values and your mission statement.

10. Introduce family to prospective teacher.
11. Create scarcity (see Nugget #44).
12. Show curriculum.
13. Give them a swag bag when they leave.
14. Ask for the enrollment.

Post-Tour:
15. Send them a thank you for touring postcard, handwritten?
16. Follow up call in 1-2 days seeing if they have any questions.
17. Capture their information in a database to market to them at a later date if they do not attend.

Make the tour checklist your own but be sure to have one so that every prospective family gets the same tour, and nothing gets forgotten. Another thing to remember is whoever does your tour needs to be the best salesperson in your company and that person may not necessarily be your director. Find the right person and train them on people and sales skills and watch your tour conversion rates climb over 50%!

NUGGET #44:
Create Scarcity

People always want what they cannot have and will pay a premium for it. Whoever does your tours needs to learn some basic sales skills, and scarcity is one of the skills that is vital to increased tour conversions.

It all starts with the phone call, which sets up the initial scarcity in the customer's mind. Let's pretend the director Jennifer receives a phone call.

Ring, ring. (Jennifer pulls out her phone script.) *"Hello, this is ABC Preschool, this is Jennifer speaking, how may I help you?"*

"Do you have openings for a two-year old?"

When asked this question there are normally two answers, yes or no. If you know there are currently five openings in that classroom, do you tell the mom that. NO!

To create scarcity here is your answer: *"There is currently only one spot available for your child, and I am getting calls every day, would you like to come in for a tour tomorrow?"*

Did she lie to the parent? Absolutely not. There is only one spot available, for <u>her</u> child.

By creating scarcity, the mom will want to tour sooner, and it will help push her to a more immediate decision because of F.O.M.O. (<u>F</u>ear <u>O</u>f <u>M</u>issing <u>O</u>ut)

You can also use scarcity to close a tour. When you get to the end of the tour and you ask for the enrollment, you may get an answer like this: *"I have to talk to my husband." "I am looking at three other schools in the area."* Blah, blah, blah.

The goal is to have this mom decide to enroll at your school quickly, so we tempt her with scarcity and F.O.M.O.

You pull a last-minute promotion out of your pocket and tell the parent that you have an expiring special offer you would like to tell her about.

Whatever you decide to give here is irrelevant, free registration, fourth week free, etc. It does not matter. What matters is the timing. Whatever offer you are enticing her with expires tomorrow at close of business. Let her know that she needs to come in and pay (based on your policy) and have paperwork done by close of business tomorrow for the promotion to be valid. This makes the parent act much quicker, and if you do not hear back from her it helps you to know how serious she was, so you don't waste much time chasing her.

So be sure to train the person who answers the phone and also the one who does the tour on the concept of scarcity. You will start seeing an increase in your tour conversions and your enrollments for sure.

NUGGET #45:
Proper Follow-Up

The biggest money loser for any child care center is improper follow up. Think about all of the work involved in getting someone to actually show up and tour your center.

Marketing dollars were spent, a phone call was received, and a tour was scheduled and given. Now you are going to drop the ball and not follow up with them?

Imagine running a 26-mile marathon and then 100 feet before the finish line you decide to quit. This is what it is like to not follow up with someone. 99% of the work has been done, but they need to hear back from you. They need to know that you care enough to see if they have any questions. Most of your competitors will not follow up, which is why you need to. Doing so will make you stand out and will help you enroll more families.

Studies have shown it takes at least seven "touches" for a person to make a buying decision. A touch is a point where the customer has either seen or heard something about your business, saw an ad, or spoke to someone at your center. A follow up call after the tour is the most important touch because it is the time where they should be best prepared to make a decision.

Make sure proper follow up is on your tour checklist and that whoever did the tour is the one who reaches back out to them 1-2 days later (if they didn't enroll on the spot). Getting good at follow up will help you to get more parents over the finish line with an enrollment at your center.

NUGGET #46:
Use Technology for Parental Communication

Today most centers have a daily communications app so that a parent can get pictures and daily reports from the school. I still come across a lot of old school owners who still make children sign in each day by hand, and I even know of one owner who still writes paychecks by hand.

Parents today are hip to new technology and as a center owner, you need to be too. Today's millennial parents are demanding this type of technology in the center that they choose. They want the ability to see what is happening with their child in real time.

There are dozens of them on the market today and I do not want to sway you one way or another. Features vary widely between platforms, so it depends on what features you are looking for. Most offer a free demo period, I would recommend trying two or three and seeing which one you like the best.

NUGGET #47:
Attend a Kris Murray Child Care Success Summit

In 2015 I read Kris Murray's amazing book *The 77 Best Strategies to Grow Your Early Childhood Program*. After reading the book I started implementing some of the strategies I learned in the book and I started seeing immediate results.

I did some more research on Kris and found that she hosted a Child Care Success Summit every year, and in 2015 it was in Orlando, Florida. I immediately purchased tickets, so my wife and I could attend.

This is the largest child care conference in the world solely focused on the business side of child care, which is the area that most center owners struggle with.

If I had to describe in one word what those three days did for my business, I would use the word *transformational*! We came back so inspired and made immediate changes in our business. The pay off was amazing as we saw revenues grow 25% in our first year!

The Child Care Success Summit happens in the fall each year, and you can get information and tickets by visiting my website http://www.childcaremillionaire.com.

NUGGET #48:
Year-Round Programs Tend to be More Profitable

Of the hundreds of child care programs that I have studied, the vast majority of the programs that were year-round programs proved to be more profitable with a higher lifetime customer value.

The vast majority of your parents will have to work all year long (unless you have a lot of school teachers at your center). Since your parents work all year long and need care all year long, why are you giving them a reason to leave you each summer or fall?

Having a parent have to register for summer camp puts a mindset into their heads that kids need to go to summer camp and they tend to start looking around at other summer camp programs.

For the past 20 years I have run a year-round program and when we enroll a new family we never mention anything about summer camp. Our rates do not change, and we do not charge them additional fees.

Having a parent re-register each year for fall enrollment has the same effect, it gives parents the mindset that they can leave since they are technically unenrolled and have to "re-enroll" with a fee. Do not give them that mindset.

My enrollment over the last 20 years has not dipped at all during summer months and my revenue has remained constant. If you have an annual dip in summer revenue you may want to consider switching to a year-round program and changing the mindset of your parents. Not having a summer camp does not mean you can't do fun stuff with the kids during the summer like taking cool field trips. Just make sure to do the fun stuff all year so they want to stick with you for the long haul.

The key is to teach the children during the summer, and market the fact that you are a year-round educational program that helps children excel when they get to school. Sell to your parents that keeping children in the same program all year is more consistent for the child and will help with emotional stability.

NUGGET #49:
Tracking Metrics

Metrics are vital to the long-term planning of your business. Fourteen years ago, I started tracking my enrollment at all my centers. I tracked full and part time enrollment in each classroom at every one of my centers. In 2015 I added full time equivalent (FTE) tracking to my data.

The more data you accumulate the more you can look for trends which will help you with planning. In the 14 years I have kept this data I started noticing that my enrollment increased sharply each year from March to June. Having that knowledge allowed us to start hiring new people each year in January and February, ahead of our anticipated growth instead of trying to play catch up after enrollment comes.

FTE is a term we use to break enrollment down to an apple to apple comparison. What I mean by that is if a classroom has a child that attends full time, that child would count as 1 FTE. The child is equal to one full-time child. Now let's look at two children that share a full-time spot. Child A attends Monday, Wednesday and Friday and pays 75% of full-time tuition. That child would count as .75 FTE. If the other child that offsets child A attends Tuesday and Thursday and pays 50% of full-time tuition the FTE would be .5. So, combined the two part time children equal 1.25 FTE whereas the full-time child was only 1 FTE.

Knowing your FTE allows you to have a good pulse on actual enrollment and will be a good indicator of how effectively you manage your part time spots. It will also always be a true indicator of revenue as well.

I had a client that was frustrated when his summer enrollment had dropped by 20 children. We put all of his numbers into an FTE Spreadsheet and he was amaze; his FTE was the same, even though his enrollment dropped by 20 children. How could this be? In the fall he lost a few staff children that were only paying 50% of tuition, and he had quite a few part time children leave and were replaced by full time children.

The result was he was making the same amount of money and had to have 2 less staff members due to 20 less children at the center.

Create a spreadsheet to track enrollment each week at your center. You will want to track all full and part time of each classroom as well as the center FTE. Doing this will make you very happy in the future when you can start identifying trends and making proactive staffing decisions instead of reactive ones.

NUGGET #50:
Reviews and Testimonials

Whenever I am about to purchase something major, the first thing I always do is look at reviews. This is one area that is very important to a child care center. There is a big difference between buying a television and trusting someone to care for your most precious commodity.

Having a weighted balance between five-star reviews and non-five-star reviews is healthy. A good rule of thumb is to try to always average 4.75 or higher. That means for every one-star review that you receive, you will need to have 19 five-star reviews to offset it.

Facebook reviews are the most susceptible to receiving a negative review. Why is that? Facebook is a platform full of people telling other people how bad they are. Social etiquette is terrible these days, with people saying things on Facebook they would never say to another person to their face.

Fill your Facebook page with positive video testimonials from your parents as news feed items. Also fill your website with positive video testimonials. By doing this it helps to offset any possible 1-star reviews that someone has left.

When a customer thinks they have been wronged, they are going to lash out today and try to hurt you, and the best way for them to do that is by telling the world on Facebook.

The good news is you can turn Facebook reviews off, so no one will see them. If you have several 1-star ratings, this is what I would recommend.

Google, Yelp, and Yahoo all have reviews that cannot be turned off, and they also cannot be changed under most circumstances. You will want to make sure you go out of your way to ask your families that love you to leave positive reviews. This will help to bury some of the not so good ones.

The best way to avoid negative reviews is to build a loyalty fence around your business, have a great personal relationship with all of your parents, be nice to everyone, and provide excellent service.

You will also want to have a written social media policy for staff as well as parents that lays out the consequences of making derogatory online statements (run this by your attorney).

Be sure to use text and video testimonials on your Facebook page, your website, on your marketing materials and in your center lobby. The more social proof you can furnish, the better you will look to a potential customer.

Encourage your satisfied customers to write a review for you on the major review sites. Some clients have held contests to increase reviews but be sure to check to see if your state will allow this. The more five-star reviews you have the better, as it will tend to drown out the inevitable one-star review you will receive from a whiny customer.

NUGGET #51:
Use 21st Century Advertising Methods

I speak to clients all of the time who still advertise in newspapers, on the radio and in local magazines. For the most part you are wasting your money when you use outdated advertising methods.

Your child care parents are mostly millennials, so why not advertise directly to them? Since the average millennial spends most of their day on their smartphone, why not spend most of your advertising dollars to reach them there.

Facebook is by far the biggest player on social media, but Instagram is also a very popular. Most of your advertising dollars should be spent on social media channels like these.

The good news for you is that Facebook owns Instagram and when you advertise on Facebook, you can set it so the ads also show up on Instagram.

To get the biggest bang for your buck I would recommend targeting your ads to women (95% of women are the decision makers on child care), ages 18-45, and you need to target parents with infants, parents with toddler, parents with preschoolers and expectant mothers (if you take infants).

By running very tightly targeted ads, you get the biggest bang for the buck even with limited funds, still reaching a good amount of people either through boosted posts or paid ads.

If you are not tech savvy, I would recommend hiring someone to do this for you. What you pay them will be worth the time, effort, and energy, and you will get a great return on your investment with these ads. You can also take a course and educate yourself on how to do them.

For the last six years, the only form of advertising I have done when looking to gain enrollments or to hire staff has been on Facebook and Instagram. The reason is simple, it works!

NUGGET #52:
Use a CRM System

I remember vividly receiving a postcard from ChildcareCRM in the mail a few years ago. The postcard sat on my desk for two years before I finally made the phone call.

I was put through to the owner of the company, Chuck Gibbs, who sold me on all of the benefits of his product. Up until that point we had an archaic pen and paper tracking system that was poorly maintained, so I knew that his product would help to modernize my business and help me track leads better.

The results were immediate, and explosive. The number of tours we received increased, our conversions skyrocketed, and our revenue went much higher.

What ChildcareCRM does is automate your parent contact mechanisms. It allows you to set up an automated email drip campaign that basically works while you sleep.

This drip campaign can send a series of automated emails and texts after you have a new lead. You can have multiple campaigns set up such as pre-tour, post-tour and post enrollment. By doing this you are customizing your message based on where your prospect is in the enrollment funnel.

If cost is stopping you from using a CRM system, you are missing the boat. One child gained due to this software will pay for this system for many years.

If you own a center and have 40 or more children enrolled, this software, or something similar, is an absolute must. I can promise you all of your major competitors have a CRM type system; where you can stand out is to have an amazing drip campaign that really grabs the reader's attention.

Since it takes the average parent seven touches from you before they make a decision, you need to be able to reach them many times. What that means is they need to hear your company name, or receive an email, text or phone call from you seven times on average before making a buying decision. If you don't want you or your director spending the whole day writing emails, texting or calling parents then this system is for you. Automation saves time and money.

The company who is able to "touch" their prospect the most often with the most effective message will usually win them as a client. Let ChildcareCRM reach out and touch leads for you. You will be glad you did.

You can get a free trial of this software by clicking on the link on my website at http://www.childcaremillionaire.com.

NUGGET #53:
Use Hand Written Notes

Technology is a double-edged sword. I must admit, Facebook has allowed me to always know when my friend's birthdays are. Every time I have a birthday, I get hundreds of Facebook messages - some from people I haven't heard from in years! I even get Facebook birthday messages from my own children. It's great that it's so easy for people to reach out with well wishes, however, I do miss getting cards and calls!

When was the last time you received a genuine hand written thank you note from someone? When was the last time you were called on your birthday by a friend? Make it a point to send handwritten thank you cards each time someone does something above and beyond.

Taking time out of our busy lives to do something no one else is doing is one of the keys to building an amazing culture at your business. Your employees and parents will love the extra attention a handwritten card will bring.

Delegate to your admin team sending out hand written thank you notes and postcards to parents as well. I require every one of my directors to send 3-5 handwritten postcards or notes to either a parent or staff member each and every week. It is no wonder why we have low staff and parent turnover at our centers.

NUGGET #54:
Recession Proof Your Business

Recession is a very scary word to most child care center owners. It has never scared me, and actually I think it is one of the best opportunities for growing your program.

Recessions on average happen around every 10 years or so. The secret to recession proofing your business lies in many of the nuggets I have shared in this book. If you will take them to heart and learn to put your business in a healthy financial position, then recession will not be scary; it will become a huge buying opportunity for you, like it was for me.

To create a recession proof business, you must first get your business in a great financial position. There are three critical things you have to do to position yourself.

1. First, debt needs to be managed properly and kept to a minimum. The more debt free you are, the better position you will be when the economy turns south.
2. Centers that you currently own need to be kept at 90% occupancy or greater to maximize profit.
3. A savings plan needs to be followed religiously and to a point of having 6 months-worth of expenses saved up.

By recession proofing your business you are preparing for the inevitable; which puts you at an advantage because your competition is probably not even thinking about it.

Recessions are all about survival of the fittest. The company with debt that is manageable and has savings that are deep will be able to outlast the competition who has not prepared themselves. As they go out of business, your business benefits in many ways. First you can pick up their children, which helps when enrollment drops by 25%. Secondly, you can hire their good staff members. Lastly, you can either acquire their center or their supplies and equipment at pennies on the dollar.

Some people will read this and think that I am heartless by advocating profiting off another person's loss. That is not what I am trying to say. If they are forced into a position of having to close down due to their own business practices and decisions, you are actually helping them out when you buy their equipment, employ their staff, and provide a place for their children to attend. In a recession there are winners and losers in all areas of the economy, I have just chosen to be a winner. I hope I am helping you to become one too.

The next time a recession hits look at it as a chance to increase your market share and grow your business, just make sure you have the right mindset and you are prepared.

NUGGET #55:
SEO: Search Engine Optimization

Your website is a great marketing tool for your business, providing it can be found by the consumer. It is far better to have an average looking website that ranks high and gets seen than an amazing website that no one gets to see. That said, if you want to crush your competition, you'll want both a website that is highly ranked by the machine algorithms of search engines AND one that impresses your prospects causing them to scramble to hit the "Book a Tour" button.

SEO can also become a significant asset in your business. Your domain name (URL) can be worth tens of thousands of dollars on its own if it ranks highly. The top three keywords in the market are Daycare, Child Care and Preschool; and the top three spots account for the majority of the traffic. If you are not ranking for these 3 keywords in the top 3 spots in your area, then you need to consider hiring a SEO specialist to craft a plan to get you more traffic. Doing so will give you much more exposure which in turn helps grow your center. http://www.childcaremillionaire.com.

NUGGET #56:
Survey Parents Annually

Sometimes the truth hurts, but it can make you a lot of money. You must be willing to ask your clients the tough questions each and every year in order for you to improve and grow.

Today's surveys are easy and inexpensive to do. There are many sites on the internet where you can create a parent survey that allows a parent to respond to you anonymously and confidentially from the comfort of their own home.

You can decide which questions you would like to ask, but make sure you ask the same questions each year. That is how you will know if you are improving or not.

Expect about a 25% response rate if you ask nicely. That should be a good basis for finding if there are some hidden issues that need to be immediately addressed. Have the mindset that for every negative comment you receive there are five other people feel the same way but haven't told you.

Make sure you ask them to tell you about all of the things they like about your program. Ask if they would refer you to a friend or relative. You may also ask them for their favorite and least favorite team member and why; that is always eye opening.

Whatever questions you pick be sure to leave a comments section at the bottom that they can write anything that is on their mind. You may not want to read some of them, but I promise you it will give you a great opportunity to improve your program *if you take action based on the results.*

A few weeks after a survey, post the results at your center along with owner comments addressing concerns and detailing your plan of action. This will help to build customer loyalty and let them know you care about their opinion.

NUGGET #57:
What Makes You Better Than the Competition?

Are you better than the center down the road? I can promise you that there is something that you do better than anyone else in your market. You need to find what that is and market it on phone calls and tours.

Put together a detailed list of the differences between you and all of your nearby competitors. In Nugget #61 I talk about mystery shopping, this is where you will get this information about your competitors and what they have to offer.

Make a brochure touting all of your unique benefits and share them to the world. Some things you may be doing better than anyone in your market: curriculum, security, parent communication apps, payment options, teacher experience, location, outdoor classroom, music, art, yoga, piano, karate, gifted program, transporting children, safety record, and inspection record.

By figuring out the 2-3 unique benefits that you do better than anyone else it puts you in a position of power when someone comes in for a tour. By always highlighting what you do the best, when the parent tours somewhere else they will remember what you said and see how others match up to you.

NUGGET #58:
Have an Attorney on Retainer

Bad things happen to good people. Good things happen to bad people. This is simply a fact of life.

To have an attorney on retainer means that you have money deposited in an attorney's trust account that you can draw upon should you need legal advice.

You need to find a reputable attorney in your area and meet with them and establish a relationship. Many will give you a free initial consultation. Ensure that they have knowledge of the state department that licenses child care centers in your state.

In my case I hired an attorney who had an incredible amount of experience dealing with state agencies. This has proven very valuable over the years.

Over the years I have faced many instances where either a staff member of mine or my center was in trouble for something and having an attorney on retainer has saved me each and every time.

I have a golden rule when it comes to my employees; if they did nothing wrong I will defend them at any cost.

Twice I have had to hire an attorney to clear the name and reputation of one of my employees. In both instances the state was trying to keep the employee from ever working in the child care industry again. Since I knew they did nothing wrong, I spent money out of my pocket defending them and clearing them of any wrongdoing.

I would recommend an immediate attorney call if any of the following happens:

1. You get served with a lawsuit.
2. A child gets seriously hurt at your center.
3. A serious licensing violation that could shut your center down.
4. Someone slandering you on social media (they can send a cease and desist letter).
5. An employee or parent says you discriminated against them.
6. You need business documents reviewed.
7. You change a company policy that you want to make sure is legal in your

state (i.e. non-compete agreement).

Attorneys are expensive, but not having one you can bounce things off of will be a lot costlier in the long run. Remember the nugget; do not step over dollars to pick up pennies. Saving a dollar here could end up costing you a fortune later.

NUGGET #59:
Licensing Inspectors Are Not the Enemy

Does it ever seem like your licensing inspector picks on you? Do they find little things that, to you, seem like no big deal? Are you stressed out each time they arrive at your center?

If you answered "yes" to any of these questions you are not alone. However, imagine if there were no licensing inspectors, or no licensing standards for that matter. What might you be tempted to change at your center? Would you increase your child-staff ratio? Would you let your employees take naps with the children? Would you let babies share bottles with each other? The answer is probably NO to *those* questions. Why? Because YOU are an amazing caregiver and you are focused on quality, but not everyone is like you.

Licensing inspectors are there to help us all maintain at least minimum levels of quality and safety for the children we are caring for and the families we are serving. I keep this in mind when I see my consultant pull up to my center, and I welcome licensing inspections. In fact, crazy as it may sound, I love my inspector. WHY? To me she is like my coach, she helps me see blind spots that I may not see in my own program. Blind spots could lead to safety concerns that could lead to a serious injury or even the death of a child. Having her input helps me stay accountable to quality and safety standards, which makes my schools more attractive to new families.

One of the biggest reasons I love my inspector is that she levels the playing field. She makes sure that everybody has to play by the same rules. For instance, I know that I have the best program in my area. I know that if my competitors have to play by the same rules that I do, I can beat them every day of the week.

It is when your competitors break the rules, and the playing field is not level, that they can undercut you on price. Imagine if the child care center down the road was adding two extra kids over ratios in each classroom. What could they do to you on price? They, most likely, would undercut you badly. Your inspector is there to keep the playing field level. They are like a referee in a football game, they exist to make sure players are safe and that everyone plays by the rules.

I have had five inspectors in the 20 years I have been in business, and I have loved every one of them. Were they tough? YES! Were they fair? YES! As long as I am treated the same as the center down the road, I am happy.

Being an inspector isn't easy, though. They are the ones that have to deal with all the hard problems, and correct centers that are breaking the rules. Because of this they aren't always met with the level of friendliness and welcoming spirit as they are met with when they visit my schools. I realize this about their job, and I strive constantly to build and maintain a positive relationship with my licensing inspectors.

Here are a couple things that I have done to help create an amazing relationship with my licensing workers.

I currently have five centers and when licensing arrives, we are immediately called and either my wife or I will run right over to do the walk through with them. I want to eyeball every infraction and be aware of everything that needs to be fixed. I want no misunderstandings about what she is asking for.

I take the items that need fixing and make sure that everything on that list is done within 24 hours (if possible). I want her to know I am responsive to safety concerns. I always take a picture of the completed work the next day and email it to her, again to show responsiveness.

I try to get to know them on a personal level. I make conversation and learn where they are from, how many kids they have, where they go on vacation, etc. I ask about these things every time I see them to show that I care about them.

I thank my inspector for everything that she hits me on, I know she is trying to keep my kids safe.

I send my worker a thank you card every so often. I let her know how much I appreciate the hard work that she does. I can promise you that no one else does this.

When interacting with your licensing inspector, show empathy. Imagine if you were in their shoes. They are responsible for the safety of the children at your center. If they let a safety concern slide, and something bad happens, they would have to live with it. Realize that they are doing the best job they can. Imagine having a job where every day you have to deal with people who more than likely hate you.

If 95% of the centers they deal with treat them negatively, and then you treat them with respect and really care for them, do you think they might treat you better? I say yes. I don't expect my inspector to ever look the other way on a safety issue, (I would never want her to) but because I have a great working relationship with her, I feel we are given the benefit of the doubt on any gray area because she knows that safety is our number one priority.

So, the next time your inspector comes knocking, greet them with a smile, ask them about their family, get to know them on a personal level. It will be like a breath of fresh air for them when you treat them with respect and maybe, just maybe, inspections won't seem quite as bad.

NUGGET #60:
Have a Parental Referral Program

Word of mouth advertising is the cheapest form of advertising, but sometimes you need to give someone a nudge to recommend you. Cash is normally a good motivator, I know it is for me.

Having a parent referral program allows a parent to recommend you in exchange for something tangible. Obviously the higher the payout, they more they may be motivated to tell their friends about your center!

Some ideas you can offer are: cash, date night (dinner and a movie with free child care), event tickets, or tuition discount. I think cold hard cash always works the best.

Whatever you choose, be sure to have a stipulation that the new family must enroll and stay at least 30 days before the referral fee is paid. You can also expand the offer to the referred family by giving them a bonus for attending. Something like: refer a friend and you both receive $200 cash after 30 days of attending our center.

NUGGET #61:
Mystery Shop Often

Once a year I hire a mystery shopper to tour all of my centers, and any nearby competitors. I want them to give me an honest assessment how I compare to the competition in many different areas.

When mystery shopping your own center be sure that your staff knows this is something that will be done at random times, so it is not unexpected and won't create negative feelings. You need to explain to staff the reason behind mystery shopping is to see what a customer sees through their eyes, which will paint a clearer picture of what your prospective clients see.

Having the same person also tour nearby competitors allows them to do an apple to apple comparison of both programs. Bottom line, you are looking for an honest opinion if the mystery shopper would attend your center or the competition and why.

Be sure to have the mystery shopper rate the following at a minimum:

1. Phone Call
2. Tour skills
3. Price
4. Cleanliness
5. Employee happiness
6. Location
7. Ease of drop off or pick up
8. Fullness of center
9. Scarcity or special offer
10. Unique benefits
11. Tour follow up

By doing this annually you will make sure that your rates are in line with what your competitors charge and also you will make sure your program is as good if not better than the competition. Never be afraid to make changes that will help you grow in the long run.

NUGGET #62:
Close for All Hands Training Days

The larger your program the more you will need opportunities to unify your team.

Having multiple centers represents a challenge when you want to make sure that everyone is on the same page. Too often employees will get tunnel vision and believe they are working for a center and not the company. Core values get harder and harder to adhere to when a center is in competition with or feel disconnected from other centers.

If you are a multi-site owner, it is very important to have all hands training days where everyone gets to meet as one big team under the same umbrella. This should be done at least every six months or so.

This is a chance to do team building exercises, to train, and to work on your core values and core focus. This is a chance for everyone to get on the same page with regards to the company mission and why you do what you do.

I have been asked many times when the best days to do these trainings are. It depends on your area, but I would recommend doing it on a weekday holiday such as President's Day or Columbus Day. The parents are paying you for the day anyway, so it really does not cost you anymore, and you can leverage the time together by posting photos on social media of staff members getting trained on a holiday.

I do have some clients who do this on a Saturday. The problem with weekends is makes for a long week for staff, plus you will have to pay overtime to the employees if they go over 40 hours.

No matter the format you use, find the time to gather the team together at least twice a year and you will begin to unify around the company's mission statement and your core values.

NUGGET #63:
Have Core Values

Core values in an organization are the guiding principles which serve as the foundation for the company's mission. Core values should substantially encompass what a company stands for and believes in.

Core values should not be created by management without the input of staff members. In Nugget #62 I talked about the importance of all hands company meetings, these are the perfect place to do core value exercises.

Ideally you want every member of your team to help create and craft your core values. Doing so will allow each team member to have buy in when crafting the ideals your company stands for.

It is up to you how you involve everyone, but in the end, you will want to come up with 3-7 core values that are a 1-3-word value. Some examples might be: fun, family, teamwork, yes, integrity.

After you come up with them you need to come up with a 1-2 sentence statement that backs up the core value. An example might be: *Fun - We make learning fun!*

Once you have figured out what core values your company stands for, it is time to brand that into your company. Use your core values on your website and in emails and post them in your center lobby.

You will want to make sure that you hire, train, discipline, reward and terminate all employees based on core values from this point forward. If an employee is not living up to the core value that they help craft, it is time for them to go. If an employee is shining and living core values every day, they need to be praised. When you hire someone, you need to show them what you stand for and make sure that they can live up to those expectations.

NUGGET #64:
Have an Ambassador of Employee and Parent Happiness

I got this nugget from a fellow coach, Jennifer Conner. At her centers she has an Ambassador of Employee and Parent Happiness.

This is not a separate job but an added responsibility for someone on your team. Empower this person with a budget and a desire to make a difference in people's lives.

This person will be the one that will send thank-you cards, sympathy cards, birthday, anniversary and congratulatory cards to employees, customers and vendors. They will send flowers, gifts, and sometimes they will just deliver a hug.

It is up to the rest of the staff to inform this person as to who needs a little love and attention each week. Make sure to pay this person a little extra for going above and beyond in this role. Just a small random act of kindness to an employee or customer can go a long way and increase retention, not to mention make someone feel a whole lot better.

CHILD CARE PROFILE

Chirag Patel

Bright Beginnings Academy

Location: New Jersey
Year Opened: 2007
# of Employees: 51
# of Locations: 2
2017 Gross Revenue: $2.6 Million

How did you finance your first location?

Purchase price was $3.8 million. SBA Financing with 25% down.

What was the biggest mistake you made in your business in the first two years?

Relying on what parents wanted and making changes not necessarily good for the entire school.

What was the smartest business decision you have ever made?

Investing in our staff and empowering our management team.

What advice would you give to someone thinking about opening or expanding a child care center?

Don't get stuck in a particular viewpoint. Many ways to be successful, just find the path that works for you financially.

Thoughts from Chirag:

For your freedom, invest in empowering your management team!

CHILD CARE PROFILE

Karla & Doug McCurry

Palm Beach Preschool

Location: Florida
Year Opened: 2007
# of Employees: 40
# of Locations: 2
2017 Gross Revenue: $2.2 Million

How did you finance your first location and what did it cost?

First location: $4.5 million, 206 capacity, 10,100 sq ft, 1.5 acres of land. Financed via SBA, conventional, 401K loan, home equity loan, and seller held a 5-year note. Second location: $1.2 million, 108 capacity, 5,200 sq ft, .5 acre of land. Financed via SBA, conventional, and seller held a 5-year note.

What are some of the biggest mistakes you made in your business in the first two years?

- *We purchased the property at too high of a price.*
- *The school was at full capacity. You can't build up. You can only maintain*

or drop.

- *Since I knew nothing about child care, having a seller who was actively involved with her school as well as loved by all the customers and inheriting a director who knew very little about managing a child care facility was a disaster.*

- *My lack of knowledge on how to motivate staff as well as effectively supervise staff.*

- *Not having my own clear vision and mission.*

- *Lack of knowledge on how to acquire and maintain customers.*

What are some of the smartest business decisions you have ever made?

Having faith in a higher power, staying true to my values, being honest, having integrity, keep persevering, and joining the Kris Murray Child Care Success Academy.

What advice would you give to someone thinking about opening or expanding a child care center?

I can't give too much advice on starting a center from scratch, but when it comes to purchasing an existing center I recommend:

- *Be patient while searching; do not purchase a center, just to purchase it. Make sure you are able to make a profit even if you were to lose a few families.*

- *Do your due diligence. Look at all financials (tuition account ledger records, attendance records, student files, staff files, payroll records, profit and loss, bank statements, income tax returns, etc.)*

- *Pull licensing records and question discrepancies. Research the school's reputation. Make sure everything lines up. If it doesn't, ask why. Do not take the seller's nor the broker's word on anything! Verify, Verify, Verify.*

- *Do not rush the sale. If the sale falls through, no worries. It wasn't meant to be and it's probably a blessing in disguise.*

Thoughts from Karla:

Everything happens for a reason. If it's meant to be, it will be.

CHILD CARE PROFILE

Linh Nguyen

Kids 'R' Kids of South Riding

Location: Virginia
Year Opened: 2016
# of Employees: 50
# of Locations: 1
2017 Gross Revenue: $2 Million

How did you finance your first location and what did it cost?

I financed my project using personal savings and investments. The project cost almost $6 Million.

What is the biggest mistake you made in your business in the first two years?

The biggest lesson I've learned is hiring right and listening to my instincts. Holding on to a management team member that does not buy into my vision caused more work for me and slowed down the company's earning potential.

What are some of the smartest business decisions you have ever made?

Treating your employees like they're your family. Take care of your very best people and they will take care your business.

What advice would you give to someone thinking about opening or expanding a child care center?

Don't sweat the small stuff, focus on your people, revenue and innovation.

Thoughts from Linh:

A positive mind finds way that it can be done. A negative mind looks for all the ways it can't be done.

Chapter 5
Management

Your management team is a very important part of your business. Developing your management team to properly lead others is a very important part of being an owner. We set the example for our managers on how we want them to lead by how we lead them. Invest in them and it will be returned to you many fold.

These following seven nuggets mostly deal with how you need to treat them, not what you should expect from them in return. In chapter six we will cover a lot about employees in general, many of those nuggets applying to management as well.

NUGGET #65:
Have a Secret Management Facebook Group

As your business grows to multiple centers it is important to make sure that the communication lines are always open. One way to get your management team on the same page is to create a secret management group on Facebook.

Having a secret group will allow you to communicate with one another in privacy away from other staff members. If you have multiple centers this will be a way for directors to speak to one another in a form where you can see the conversations and can help control the narrative.

This is a place where you can reiterate policy, pass on instructions, and communicate with your team. Be careful to keep this page positive and never criticize someone in this forum - that would be bad. On the other hand, be sure to publicly praise someone or everyone in this forum.

There are also other workplace communication apps and software that will allow you to be more efficient in the workplace.

NUGGET #66:
Never Micro-Manage

Leadership is defined as the ability to influence others, it does not mean bossing people around or controlling every move of someone that works for you.

All too often in the child care industry owners have zero business or leadership training anywhere in their life and it leads to serious problems as your business grows.

I have had clients with varied backgrounds. Some were teachers, lawyers, pharmacists, engineers, accountants, nurses and many children of child care owners. The one thing the clear majority of them had in common, they were never properly trained in how to lead others at any point in their life.

Most of the problems with the management in your organization will stem from the owner's lack of leadership skills. An owner's weakness in leadership will transcend easily to a director and assistant director and then suddenly they will have problems leading others.

Micro-management is one of the areas that is a killer of independent thought and creative thinking. Having someone dictate your every move when you are supposed to be trusted with the responsibility of leading others is demeaning and deflating. Eventually that leader will quit or will become your puppet and then you will be the actual leader, and that is not healthy to the growth of an organization.

One problem that owners with no leadership training face is that no one will ever be you. Very few people will ever have the work ethic you have, very few will work as hard as you do, and very few will be as dedicated to your core values and mission statement as you. This is okay! You need to learn to accept 85-90% of your commitment as perfectly acceptable. If you keep demanding your team to be as committed as you are, life will become very frustrating as this person will almost never be found.

Build leaders up by properly training them in all areas I am discussing in this chapter; leadership, sales and customer service. You as the owner need to be trained in all these areas as well, and you need to lead by example. Learn to accept the fact that people make mistakes.

NUGGET #67:
Invest in Sales Training

Those who answer the phone and do tours at your center, as well as the owner all need to be trained in sales skills. Look up the definition of sales in the dictionary and tell me you are not selling a very high-priced commodity - you are.

A phone call sells a tour. A tour sells an enrollment. Good customer service skills help to sell a customer from potentially leaving. Everyone on your leadership team needs to be trained in how to sell with passion and purpose.

The most successful salespeople are passionate about the product or service that they are selling. Their enthusiasm shows in their words and their actions. They have empathy and can see things from a customer's perspective.

Send your team to sales training and you will get that money back many times over. There are many online training courses as well. All it takes is a mindset shift and a little bit of training and watch your tour conversions go through the roof!

NUGGET #68:
Develop the Leaders Around You

Besides providing training in sales and customer service, your leadership team needs to be highly trained in the areas of leadership and personal development.

Leadership is the ability to influence others towards a common objective. Everything in your company will be influenced positively and negatively by leadership, or lack thereof. Leadership is also about setting the example. A boss says *"I,"* a leader says *"We."* A boss says *"Go,"* a leader says *"Let's go."* Be a leader not a boss.

People leave managers, they seldom leave a company. People follow leaders, they do not follow titles. Poor leadership skills of owners, directors and assistant directors creates a toxic workplace and causes high amounts of turnover. I have read it takes about $4,000 to properly train a teacher in our industry. Being stingy on providing leadership and personal development training to your management team will cost you dearly.

If you are experiencing high turnover at your center, do not always point to pay as the reason. People stay where they are appreciated and where their contribution makes a difference. They also want to work somewhere that is run by a leader worthy of following.

In Nugget #101 I give a list of recommended books that will help you develop yourself and the leaders around you. I would recommend getting Audible® and listening to leadership books every day on your commute to and from work. You will be amazed at how much you will grow and change by taking non-productive time and making it productive!

NUGGET #69:
Bonus Your Leadership Team

Bonusing your leadership team is a great way to have them take ownership in your program. "Sharing the profits" helps them to feel like they are responsible for the success of the business and helps with "buy-in".

There are many ways which you can bonus your director, assistant director and other admin team members. I would recommend tying many of them to performance and profitability of the center.

Create benchmarks that they will be bonused on, areas such as:

1. Tour conversion
2. Phone script usage
3. Tour checklist usage
4. Tour conversions
5. CRM Usage
6. Mystery shopping results
7. Employee or customer satisfaction
8. Employee turnover
9. Parent retention
10. Company profits

Although it is up to you how often bonuses are given out, I recommend giving them out quarterly rather than monthly or annually. It will be easy to look at the quarter and see how the center is doing and be able to bonus based on the results. Make sure that there is a clear benchmark and when it is achieved, the bonus is paid.

NUGGET #70:
Develop a "Farm Team"

When I was a little kid I can remember going to hockey games of a local "farm team" of the New York Rangers NHL team. The farm team is where hockey players who are not quite skilled enough to make it to the big leagues are developed and trained until they are "called up" to the big leagues.

I have opened nine centers over the last 20 years and I have never hired a director or assistant director off the street with an advertisement, every one of them were hired from within. I worked hard to develop a talented pool of leaders so that when they were "called up" they were ready, willing and able to jump right in.

These future leaders need to know that they are in your management training program. They will need to be given added responsibilities, trained heavily, and allowed to be supervised in the roles you are training them for. Another thing developing future leaders does is it never puts you in a position where someone has leverage over you. I hear it a lot from clients that tell me they cannot let go of a horrible director because they have no one to replace them. Never allow this to happen, spend a little extra money developing them now knowing that someday you will need them.

The best luck I have had is from young, educated hard working teachers who never saw themselves as a director. I test employees in leadership early to see if they have natural ability, or to see if they could be taught to lead. Once I identify a potential leader I always reward them with more responsibility, tell them what my plan for their leadership training is and I put a plan into action. Almost every time they live up to my expectations and are flattered that I saw something in them that they never saw in themselves. This has helped me to build an amazing team of loyal, dedicated, hardworking directors and assistant directors who help to run my centers.

NUGGET #71:
Empower Leaders to Make Decisions

The more you empower your team to make decisions the more freedom you will have from having to make them. The smaller the business, the more likely it is that you are making all the decisions.

As your business grows you need to be able to empower your team to make decisions that you just don't have time to make. You also want them to be able to make timely decisions that can be the difference between a customer being upset all weekend or a director resolving it at pickup on a Friday evening.

As you empower them with decision making and with budgetary items, have pre-set parameters that they can operate in without having to run it by you. The more power you can trust others with the more freedom you will have. Make sure that you are kept in the loop on important issues at your weekly meetings.

As your program expands to multiple centers you can build in layers of responsibility, decision making and control over certain areas of the business. It is impossible to run multiple centers and still have control over all areas of the business. The more delegation and empowerment that is given to staff, the bigger the business can grow and the more time you will be able to spend on high payoff activities like growing your business.

CHILD CARE PROFILE

Donna Jensen

The Learning Station CDC LLC

Location: South Carolina
Year Opened: 2003
# of Employees: 34
# of Locations: 2 (second location coming in fall of 2018)
2017 Gross Revenue: $1.5 million

How did you finance your first location and what did it cost?

We rented a facility that was an old boot store. We remodeled it spent about $25,000 initially but it was like throwing money into a money pit. We moved to a location three years later to a facility designed to be a center and it was the best decision ever.

What was the biggest mistake you made in your business in the first two years?

Trying to renovate a building that wasn't designed to be a child care center. Licensing, fire, DHEC were constantly throwing obstacles in our way to get our license. We had to keep spending money we weren't expecting to spend. It was a tough start! I would also add that trying to do everything myself and not delegating was exhausting!

What are some of the smartest business decisions you have ever made?

Ramping up my administrative team. Having enough people to do everything with excellence allowed us to grow and our income far exceeded the cost of extra staff. I would also say being part of groups with other owners to be able to brainstorm ideas and keep current on trends.

What advice would you give to someone thinking about opening or expanding a child care center?

Find a reliable mentor/coach. Don't be afraid to ask questions, there are no dumb questions in this field. We have experienced it all or know someone who has! Never ever take a waiting list for granted, you don't know when a situation will arise and you will need to fill vacancies. Do your due diligence and check everything out. Building and licensing will always take longer than you expect.

Thoughts from Donna:

If you don't help them grow, you will watch them go... love your staff so you don't lose them!!

CHILD CARE PROFILE

Sharon Foster

Bells Ferry Learning Centers

Location: Georgia
Year Opened: 2001
# of Employees: 60
# of Locations: 5
2017 Gross Revenue: $1.386 Million

How did you finance your first location?

Purchase price was $1.3M. I used a combination of a small seller note ($35K) plus a $125K loan against the FF&E for the down payment on an SBA loan for the balance.

What was the biggest mistake you made in your business in the first two years?

I was completely undercapitalized. I did not have enough money in reserve to operate during growth mode. As a result, I went deeper and deeper into debt to keep the doors open until the center became profitable. I opened a home equity line and, over time, owed more on that than the original mortgage balance. Happy to say that it was paid off several years ago but the stress of watching that balance grow was massive.

What was the smartest business decision you have ever made?

Honestly – and I don't mean this as just flattery – joining Kris Murray's Child Care Success Academy made a huge difference in my business. Kris has said herself, "If you don't get coaching from me, get if from somewhere." Just having someone who can guide, advise, and share has an incredible impact. So many of us in the child care industry are here because we love children and are knowledgeable in child development. Those aren't skills that translate well to making sound business decisions. A business coach can help guide decision-making while the child care owner can continue to focus on making improvements that benefit the children.

What advice would you give to someone thinking about opening or expanding a child care center?

Learn how to balance your decision-making by combining the best interests of the children with the best interests of the business. They are not mutually exclusive. You can benefit both. But the minute you start to put either one as a priority over the other consistently, you are on a path to failure.

Thoughts from Sharon:

It's my job to make the staff happy. It's their job to make the children happy. If we are all doing our jobs, we will have happy parents. Happy staff + happy children + happy parents = child care success.

And I've always loved something Pat Vinson, founder of Kids 'R' Kids said to me once: "There isn't a problem in the world that 10 more kids can't solve."

CHILD CARE PROFILE

The Parag Family

(Vic & Aarti Parag and Kamal & Manisha Parag)

Kids' Zone Daycare & Learning Center

Location: Georgia
Year Purchased: 2016
# of Employees: 32
#Locations: 1
2017 Gross Revenue: $1.4 Million

How did you finance your first location and what did it cost?

$1.8 million, financed by bank loan.

What was the biggest mistake you made in your business in the first two years?

- *Not being confident enough to express our values and vision so they are carried out from day 1, since we did not have prior child care experience.*

- *Allowing the tail to wag the dog.*

What are some of the smartest business decisions you have ever made?

- *Joining the Kris Murray Child Care Success Academy and other professional networking organizations!*

- *Disassociating ourselves with employees who did not buy into our vision.*

What advice would you give to someone thinking about opening or expanding a child care center?

- *Keep a very close eye on operating costs, and be in an area where you are able to charge a higher tuition fee.*

- *It's easy to be drawn into the weeds and lose sight of the bigger picture. Every now and again, take a step back.*

Thoughts from Vic & Kamal:

- *Always have a growth mindset and ask your teachers to have the same.*

- *Be as transparent as you can with your teachers about your school.*

- *Remember in child care – it's a marathon, not a sprint.*

Chapter 6
Employees

Employees are the lifeblood of any organization. You would not have a business without them. In this chapter we will discuss many ideas from hiring to firing, from policies to boundaries. These nuggets will help you have a good foundation on how to deal with the most complex part of your business, employees.

Most of you who are reading this book were never taught how to lead people. The military trained me extensively in this area. Seldom do colleges teach you how to have people work for you, most teach you how to go work for someone else.

If you have done a poor job at leading others in the past, you are not alone. The good news is it all changes today. These nuggets will arm you with some techniques and if you couple them with some of my recommended reading on leadership in Nugget 101 you will be well on your way to successfully influencing and leading others.

NUGGET #72:
Have a Secret Staff Facebook Group

The ability to get a message to your entire team very quickly is one of the biggest reasons to have a secret staff Facebook group. The term "secret" refers to the privacy level setting - you will want it secret, so no one will know who your employees are, especially your competitors.

This page will also be a great place to share positive messages and for teachers to post things. Be sure to never criticize anyone individually in the group, but it is okay to praise individually inside the group.

Some of the things you can post would be: Positive messages, announcements, training videos, links to blogs or articles, reminders, celebrations, praise and fun. Teacher networking is a great feature that they will love.

In a future nugget I explain the importance of getting cell phones out of the classroom, so be sure that they are not checking, liking or commenting when they are supposed to be watching children, but they can do so on their break or off-time.

We have had this group set up for many years at our centers and the employees love engaging with each other. It has been a great resource for us to get a message out quickly and efficiently. It is free and only takes a few minutes to set up.

NUGGET #73:
Be Quick to Terminate a Toxic Employee

Just like cancer can spread quickly through a body, a toxic employee can spread a cancer-like atmosphere to your culture in a very short timeframe.

A negative attitude of a toxic employee can quickly spread to others, especially in today's social media culture. You must cut the cancer out of your organization quickly or it could kill the business.

By having a strong set of core values you are able to hold employees accountable to a set of standards that were created by the whole team. Once core values are not lived up to by a staff member, it is time to let that person go. Tolerating this behavior gives a green light to everyone else that this behavior is acceptable, and it will spread very quickly. Once parents start seeing it they will begin pulling their children out.

Make sure that you keep detailed documentation of all behavior that warrants termination, especially if this person is from a protected class. Document everything with witness statements and write-ups and always give the employee a chance to correct the behavior before letting them go. Make sure the write-up clearly lays out what will happen if there is no improvement and be sure to have them sign it.

NUGGET #74:
Have a Social Media Policy

Having a strong social media policy for employees and parents is very important as your business grows.

In today's world social media can be an incredible tool to reach a lot of people with your message for zero or very little dollars, or it can be a destructive force that can damage your brand very quickly.

Your employees will more than likely be social media junkies when they join your program. They will more than likely be used to spending the good part of their day liking posts and seeing what their friends are posting to social media.

Social media has shaped younger generations sense of identity and painted everyone else's world as perfect at the expense of our own. We seldom show the world our true self on social media, but also seldom realize that others are doing the same thing. We tend to see that others seem to have everything going right for them while we suffer in silence.

Understanding your employees need for validation through likes and the number of friends they have will help you to be able to work with this type of person.

When you hire someone, it is very important to sit down with them and explain your social media policy. New people will be going through social media withdrawals for the first few weeks and will often either sneak their cell phone into their classroom or take extra bathroom breaks to check likes and posts. Make sure they know the consequences of breaking your social media policy.

Some things you will want to put in your policy (check with an attorney in your state for legalities of regulating social media).

1. Employees are not allowed to be social media friends with customers.
2. Posts relating to anything negative that happened at work are not allowed.
3. Employees are not allowed to respond negatively to anyone else's posts about anything that happens at the center.
4. Employees are not allowed to send graphic, sexual, or other inappropriate messages to fellow employees.
5. Posts that are negative to any employee, owner, customer or child are not allowed.
6. Posts mentioning customer or children's names are not allowed.
7. Derogatory comments towards the center, owners or fellow employees will be met with legal action post-employment.

I do not want to regulate what they post on their own page - if they want to post foolish drunken photos I could care less. If they do choose to post foolish photos that aren't in line with the values of my center, I do not allow them to add my center as their place of work to their Facebook page. That is clearly stated in my policy when hired.

You will want to make sure you have a policy that protects you against negative posts by your parents as well. They need to be held to the same standard of conduct and know that you will take legal action when faced with vicious slander of your brand via social media.

Make sure you reinforce that your company policy forbids being friends on social media platforms with employees of the company. This will help them to understand why friend requests are being ignored.

Being strict with your social media policy will help to eliminate a lot of problems that can arise. Never worry about being the bad guy here, you have worked hard to build a reputable brand and simply cannot risk it being tainted.

NUGGET #75:
Get Cell Phones out of the Classroom

If you allow your staff members to have a cell phone in the classroom you are asking for trouble that could potentially shut your center down.

Studies have shown that when a person is on a cell phone they get tunnel vision and actually lose their peripheral vision. Have you ever been on a cell call while driving and then drive right past your exit, or forgot to take a turn? This is what I am talking about.

If a cell conversation can cause us to miss an exit we have taken every day for years, imagine what will happen if a child is choking, or having a seizure. The teacher may easily miss a life-threatening situation because she is focused on how many likes she is getting on her latest post.

If I was a prospective parent and I saw a teacher on a cell phone when he or she was supposed to be watching children, I would not take my children to that center. How many children have you lost because of your policy? If you are allowing your teachers to text parents, well that crosses a huge boundary line. I would much rather you get a parent communication app that does not allow real time teacher communication.

Boundaries can be blurred as well when your employees start becoming "friends" with parents on social media platforms. You do not want your parents seeing pictures of one of your employees running around drunk in their underwear on Facebook, I can promise you that.

NUGGET #76:
Have a Non-compete and Non-disclosure Agreement

You will spend a lot of money training a new hire to your way of caring for children, so you need to make sure this person can't take your training and use it against you by leaving to work for a competitor.

I recommend having a non-compete agreement with all your staff members, especially your director and assistant director.

The biggest reason you need a non-compete clause is to prohibit a staff member from directly competing with you by starting a child care center of their own. You will want it to have a distance limitation and a time limitation. "Employee is forbidden from directly competing with employer within 30 miles and for two years after employment".

You will also want to limit their ability to work for another employer, since they have been privy to your trade secrets that can be used against you. "Employee is forbidden from being employed by a business that directly competes with employer within 20 miles and for one year after employment".

You need to protect yourself from your employee's potentially leaving your center and sharing confidential information with your competitors. You will need a non-disclosure agreement (NDA) to prohibit the sharing of your expansion plans, profitability, curriculum, client list, financial information or any other trade secrets that you wish to protect.

Be sure to check with an attorney licensed in your state for the legality of aforesaid documents in your state. Knowing how hard it is to keep and retain quality staff, you will sleep better knowing they can't run to your competitor next door if they offer them a dollar more an hour.

NUGGET #77:
Treat Employees Right

If you expect your employees to work hard and give their best every day they need to be treated well and compensated fairly.

Compensation does not always have to be in the form of hourly wages, it can also come in benefits, bonuses, paid time off and insurance benefits.

Be sure that you are competitive in the marketplace and do not be afraid to raise rates on your parents to give your staff members a raise. I raise my rates annually and tell all my parents the exact percentage of the increase that will go to increased staff wages. When a parent knows that their $10 extra a week is helping their child's teacher to put a few more dollars in his/her pocket, the objections are usually non-existent.

You must also be sure you are treating employees with respect and developing a team atmosphere with core values. Remember that employees follow a leader they respect, they will rarely follow a title. Employees do not care how much you know until they know how much you care. Take a genuine interest in your people and watch productivity go through the roof.

My friend and colleague, Sindye Alexander, has written a book, **Relationship Roadmap**: *Real-World Strategies for Cultivating a Positive and Collaborative Culture in Your Preschool* which will help you with several strategies for treating your employees well.

NUGGET #78:
Success with Millennials

Clients often tell me that it is next to impossible for them to work with millennials. I hear stories about them being lazy, wanting constant approval and of them being unreliable. What is happening is a communication gap. The more of an age gap between the owner and the employee, the more of a probability of them not being able to see eye to eye on a lot of things.

If you are over 45 you cannot fathom the constant need to spend each moment of every day glued to your cell phone to see who is liking your posts. You also cannot understand why you would want everyone to know everything you are doing, where you are always going, and how you're feeling while doing it.

If you are of an older generation, you would do well to study the topic of successfully leading and managing millennials. Knowing how they think is the key to how to successfully motivate them. Millennials have grown up in a different world than it was 40 years ago. Society has molded this generation to be more plugged in to technology, and more concerned with social matters than other generations. Knowing what motivates them is the key to successfully integrating them into your team and helping them become a valued member of your staff.

Millennials thrive on feeling like they are part of something bigger than themselves, they want to work for a good cause. A sense of why is very important to them, and if you have a strong core value system it will resonate with them.

The paycheck is not the reward to a millennial, it is just a way for them to afford their cell phone, rent and tattoos. A pat on the back or a *"Thank you very much for the hard work!"* goes a lot further with them - it is equivalent to 1000 likes on their social media post. Write a handwritten note to them and they will work extra hard for you.

Look for leaders amongst your millennial ranks. Of all the directors I have had in my 22 years in the business, 95% of them were millennials and they were by far some of the best I have seen in the industry. Giving them a chance at leadership at a young age when others wouldn't will develop a sense of loyalty to you and your company that will result in them staying with you for a long time.

NUGGET #79:
Trust...but Verify.

One of my favorite sayings from President Ronald Reagan was *"Trust, but verify."* President Reagan said this to Mikhail Gorbachev upon signing of the INF treaty.

What would *trust but verify* mean to a child care center owner? It means don't end up like the dozens of owners I have met over the years who have been robbed blind by employees whom they trusted but never verified.

You must have systems in place to keep employees from stealing from you. Food, diapers, toilet paper, and supplies go missing every day from centers across the world and the owners have no clue it is going on.

You need to have systems in place to be on the lookout and catch employee theft. Inventory stock often and look for things that are out of the ordinary.

Directors have the highest probability of becoming a child care thief by a term I call ghosting. This means taking cash for a child but not officially registering them into the program. This happens at multisite centers more often or centers where an owner is not present in the day to day. Smaller centers without electronic sign in programs are more likely to experience this.

To prevent your center from being robbed, put dual integrity checks in place. Things which require more than one person to input the same data as to be able to spot irregularities.

I have had only one director steal from me (that I know of), but she did not consider it stealing. She was taking payments one week and not giving them to me until 2-3 weeks later and using those payments to help float her home rent. I caught it when I confronted a parent about non-payment and she showed me her receipt for payment which was never turned in. She was fired immediately and quickly paid me in full to keep the police out of it.

Moving most of your parents to ACH payment will help to avoid these issues, but there are always ways a creative thief will devise to part you from your money. Always have checks and balances in your program and a reward system to employees who report theft, waste, or abuse.

NUGGET #80:
Hire Smartly and Decisively

We always talk about being slow to hire and quick to fire, but this does not work in a super low unemployment economy.

You are better off hiring them and letting them go in the first 30 days if they don't work out. In most states, that will not affect your unemployment rating. By waiting an extra few days, your competitor may make them an offer and you lose a potential superstar teacher. You can make them a conditional offer dependent on passing a background and reference check.

NUGGET #81:
Reducing Interview No-Shows

The number one complaint I hear from clients these days is staffing. At the time of this book printing, the US economy is booming and unemployement is at a record low, so attracting quality staff and keeping them is getting harder and harder as employers have been raising wages and incentives to attract staff at a higher rate than we can raise parent tuition.

It is time to get pro-active and start fighting back! I have developed these techniques over the past 20 years and now boast a very small no-show percentage and a very low turnover rate, in an area with less than 3% unemployment.

In the electronic world it is possible to send out hundreds of resumes with one click. The result from this you get is a stack of applicants that did not have much invested in applying to work at your center. Make them come to you and prove how serious they are. Require (or highly encourage) all applications or resumes to be delivered in person. These will be your most serious applicants.

Having them come in person accomplishes several things.

1. They know where you are located and cannot use the "I got lost on my way to the interview" excuse.
2. You know they have reliable transportation.
3. A picture is worth a thousand words! How many times have you interviewed someone who looked good on paper and when they arrived you knew within

five minutes they would not be a good fit for your program but felt obligated to finish the interview thus wasting your time?

4. They get to see your program in action.

If you are not comfortable requiring all applicant to apply in person, another option is to do a video conference with all prospective applicants prior to the formal interview. When you have a promising application, set up a 5-10-minute pre-qualification interview. This will see how good they are at showing up on time, you can size them up and ask qualifying questions, and determine if the person is worthy of an extended interview. This also works well for applicants who are not in your area - you can do the entire interview over a video conference.

Have your director size them up by having a pre-interview questionnaire ready to ask each person that drops off an application. Use a numbering type system based on criteria that you decide and say an applicant is an 8 or above (or whatever benchmark you choose) have the director schedule an interview with the one who makes hiring decisions (within 24 hours).

You will want to look at appearance, demeanor, qualifications, attitude, hygiene, and how they answer your pre-interview questions to determine how you move forward. Using a number rating system allows you to prioritize your interviews and allows you to not waste your time on anyone that ranks low on your numbering system.

NUGGET #82:
Always Audition New Applicants

Most states will allow you to audition a new staff member providing they are supervised and not counted towards child-staff ratios. There are several things you are looking for. Are they a self-starter or do they need constant direction? Do they get on the floor and engage children at their level? Do they enjoy themselves? Are they a little goofy with the kids? Did they have fun?

Create a checklist to rate each candidate and be sure that the same teacher does all your auditions to ensure that all candidates are judged equally.

Upon completion of the audition make a hiring decision right away and get them started. The longer you procrastinate the more chance a good applicant can be swayed away from a better offer.

Be sure to check with an attorney and your licensing worker as to the legalities of auditioning a new staff member. You may have to pay this person in some states and in others it may not be allowed without successful passing of background checks.

NUGGET #83:
Invest in Your Rising Stars

The money you invest in your staff's education is never wasted. Education is one of those things that will pay dividends for the rest of your life.

Be sure that you have a policy for reimbursing or paying for further training for your staff members, especially training that will lead them to have the ability to lead others. Make sure there are caveats that specify what would have to be paid back if an employee left within a certain period.

Helping someone who has leadership skills that could be a director or assistant director for you at some point in the future to get a CDA or a degree helps to keep stability in your business. The more director qualified employees in the ranks of your business the less chance for instability when your director or assistant director gives notice.

When crafting your budget, be sure to allot a certain amount of money to invest in your people, I can promise you it will be a return on investment that will not be matched anywhere else.

NUGGET #84:
Survey your Staff Annually

The reason most employers do not survey their staff annually is that they are afraid at what they will say.

Never fear the unknown when the known can save you time, money and aggravation. The more you know about the pulse of your employees the better your center will run and the happier your employees will be. You will be amazed at how happy your staff will be by just asking them for their opinion.

Every year you need to do a survey where staff can respond either electronically or via paper to a survey you have created. You want them to know that you wish them to be open and honest and that you will read each answer with an open mind. Be sure to keep your word in this regard.

What you ask is up to you but be sure to ask questions on a scale instead of essay type replies, they will be much easier to score year to year to judge improvement.

For example, you may want to ask on a scale on 1-10 how likely would you be to recommend our center to a friend or relative. Another question might be how likely are you to still be working here one year from now?

Asking these same questions year after year will allow you to see if your culture is improving or getting worse by looking at the average score in all your categories. I would recommend limiting the survey to 10 questions and have a comments section at the bottom for them to write anything they wish. Be sure to address the comments in a company-wide memo unless the comment should not be repeated. Doing so will show everyone you took the time to listen and respond.

NUGGET #85:
Have a Staff Referral Program

The lowest rate of no shows will be from employee referrals. Your employees have a lot of friends. They talk about their job when they are around them.

Offering a cash incentive for employees to refer a friend who comes to work is a great way to find good employees. Make sure the bonus is tied to a timeframe, say after the person works for 90 days, then the bonus is paid out.

When you post an ad on a social media platform ask all your employees to like it and share it to their pages. This will help you to get maximum exposure for all help wanted ads and help employees to get a referral fee for someone who saw their shared post.

NUGGET #86:
Set Clear Boundaries

Employees and customers do not mix outside of the teacher and parent relationship and doing so is a recipe for major problems in your program.

There are several areas where clear boundaries need to be established. They are:

- Employees babysitting for parents.

- Employees communicating with parents after hours.

- Employee signing out children and transporting them home.

- Social media postings.

- Who employees are allowed to friend on social media.

- Dating of co-workers or parents.

- Outside employment by employees (I know of one client who had teachers who were strippers as a second job).

Having a clear written policy will protect you from things that will come back and bite you, I can promise you that. Be sure to be consistent in your enforcement and never apologize for being strict with setting clear boundaries.

NUGGET #87:
Employee Rewards and Incentives

Salary alone will not excite your employees, there needs to be something else to reward them for the hard work and dedication to the job.

I hear it a lot, especially from owners that have been around a while, that new employees just don't seem to be motivated by money.

Rewarding today's employees for hard work and dedication to their job is not as easy as it used to me. In the old days you worked an hour and expected to be paid for an hour. Today's workers do not have the same work ethic and are motivated differently than in the past.

In today's social media world, everyone is craving attention. Likes from friends are the validating currency of today, where in the past it has always been about the dollar. You must recognize this and adjust your thinking accordingly.

Giving all employees a $10 gift card to Starbucks may seem like a great gesture, but to an employee who hates coffee it is an insult. Giving someone a $50 gift card to a nice steakhouse seems like an incredibly nice gesture, but to a vegan it is anything but.

Rewarding employees does not need to be expensive. I remember when one of my director's hand wrote a personal note to each employee while including a $2 bill in an envelope. The note read, "You are as unique as a $2 bill and we really appreciate all that you do."

The secret to rewarding employees is to know them on a personal level, and that takes incredible leadership and people skills. Know their hot buttons, their likes and dislikes, their hobbies, their favorite beverages, their favorite restaurant. How do you find out this information? Ask them! When I onboard a new employee, we ask them these questions as we get to know them. By having this information, I am able to tailor my reward and incentive system to things that an employee actually likes, not what we think they like.

No matter how you reward employees for doing an amazing job; whether it be with time off, cash, gift cards, spa certificates or the owner's parking spot, be sure to do something. These amazing employees could have chosen to work for anyone, and they chose you to believe in. Believe in them in return and you will see productivity increase and turnover decrease.

NUGGET #88:
Onboarding

You have spent considerable time and money to get an applicant in the door. You interviewed several people and have narrowed it down to the one you have chosen. Do not blow it now, you have already done the hard part.

Proper onboarding is vital to new employee retention in the first 30-90 days. This is the time where we can really lay the groundwork for an amazing long-term employee, or we can quickly make them regret the decision and continue to do interviews with your competitors.

The first day is all about making them feel welcome. Do not rush to put them into a classroom, there is plenty of time for that. Spend time introducing them to each employee and having them take a few minutes for each of them to learn a little about one another. This is very important for two reasons; it helps the new employee feel connected to co-workers and it also allows the current staff member to have a connection with someone who will be causing some stress in the center for a few weeks.

New employees are stressful to a well-run center. The less turnover you have, the more problems that will be created when you onboard a new employee. Imagine you have a team of 6-10 employees that function amazingly as a team, they know what to do without being told, they help each other out, they all know what they are doing.

Now comes someone that knows nothing about how things are done. This person does not know where the mop is, does not know what time the kids eat, they do not know where the restroom is, they do not know what child injury procedures are at your center. Basically, they know very little.

This causes stress on the operation, but many owners fail to realize that the new employee is rarely at fault here.

One way to avoid these problems is to have an amazing onboarding and mentoring program. Doing so will give the new employee time to learn the ropes in a more controlled setting without upsetting the status quo too much.

One thing we have done is create a competency checklist that a new employee must complete within 30 days of hire. Only certain employees are allowed to work with new employees and train them. Everything on the list are items that need to be demonstrated to the trainer or mentor in order to have them signed off. After the 30 days we know they are proficient enough to be placed working with any staff member.

NUGGET #89:
Have a Mentorship Program

One of the biggest reasons a new employee will quit is they never felt like they belonged to the team. I believe improper onboarding of new staff members is one of the biggest mistake's employers make.

Think about all the money you spend to get a new employee in the door. Staff time to create advertisements, the cost of ads, staff time calling applicants, staff time interviewing applicants and staff time onboarding them.

All that money spent and then you throw them to the wolves and wish them luck. The wolves are the other employees that have been working well as a team until the new person showed up. A new person means many questions being asked and it means more work for everyone else training that person to a new way of doing things. Very seldom do fellow employees get super excited about training a new person to work with.

Having a staff mentorship program helps bridge the gap between owner/management and your new hire. The mentor is someone your new hire can go to with questions; a friendly face to teach the ropes of the center and be sure they are welcomed in with open arms. The mentor introduces the new hire around to everyone and makes sure that there is acceptance from everyone on the team.

The first day is the scariest which is probably why many of you have had a new person go to lunch on day one and not return. Make the first day special with a welcome to the team gift basket or something else special to make them feel welcome. After the first week the mentor needs to sit down with them and answer questions and see if there are any problems.

I would recommend the mentor taking them out to lunch on their 30-day anniversary. Celebrate that milestone by making them feel special. If someone is going to quit it is usually going to be around the one-month mark, so this lunch will help you to identify issues before they become issues.

Having a mentorship program will lower your staff turnover in the first 90 days and will help you to have employee buy in earlier in their career working with you.

Make sure you pick the right person for this job, it needs to be someone that loves people and is good at training. Consider a small bonus for the mentor if a new employee stays 180 days. I would be a nice gesture that will reward them for helping you create longevity with new employees.

CHILD CARE PROFILE

Lucy Cook, Bruce Mazey, & Phil Mazey

Amaze Education

Location: Australia
Year Opened: 2008
# of Employees: 130
# of Locations: 9
2017 Gross Revenue: $7.5 Million AUD ($5.3 Million USD)

How did you finance your first location?

Bank loan – no one would touch us because we had no assets (originally Phil/Alison and me). The evening before the business settled the loan manager rang to tell us his superiors had refused us, after being told all the way along everything would be fine. I was able to talk them into us, though they required extra deposit. Phil's dad Bruce came on as a partner.

What are some of the biggest mistakes you made in your business in the first two years?

- *Hiring a bad accountant. She didn't have the right experience and did not do the due diligence on the first business properly. If she had, we never would have bought it. It was run down, had poor occupancy and was licensed for 64 children a day but could only fit in 50 because of the size of the classrooms.*

However, if we had known all this, we never would have bought it and our journey would not have begun.

- *Hiring the wrong director – we lost 17 families in one year. The hiring was not the problem, it was not letting her go fast enough. Make sure your director fits in with your culture.*

What was the smartest business decision you have ever made?

- *Saying yes then working out the details later.*
- *Building our business on relationships, children, families, staff, community.*
- *Living our culture, breathing our vision.*
- *Learn where your strengths lie and outsource what you struggle with.*
- *Follow any period of growth with a period of stability, your processes, everything, needs time to catch up. Growth is uncomfortable and it does take a while to grow into the way your company now is.*

What advice would you give to someone thinking about opening or expanding a child care center?

- *Imagine how hard you think you will need to work, multiply by 80 and that's about right.*
- *Surround yourself with great people, accountants, lawyers, bank manager, other owners and so on.*
- *Your staff are your best asset and can be your greatest downfall.*
- *Childcare is never stable, you can lose a family, have a serious incident and a staff issue all before morning tea then the next day three enrolments walk through the door. You do get used to the swings and roundabouts.*
- *Never stop growing – be committed to growth and learning.*

Thoughts from Lucy:

Fear is never a reason for inactivity. Every day is a new day.

CHILD CARE PROFILE

Sholom Strick

Northlight Childcare Management

Location: Illinois
Year Opened: 2010
# of Employees: 100
#Locations: 8
2017 Gross Revenue: $4,380,354

How did you finance your first location?

My father owned a building that was formerly a church and garage, we combined it to one big unit of about 5000 feet. He helped me by financing the renovations, buying materials, etc...

What was the biggest mistake you made in your business in the first two years?

Probably focusing too much on enrollment and less on building a quality team and reputation from within.

What are some of the smartest business decisions you have ever made?

Take some risks once you are at a certain comfort level. I opened a location based on my gut feeling about a neighborhood and it turned out to be our best area for growth. Sometimes you'll never know if you don't try. And if you turn out to be wrong, you'll learn just as much from that too.

What advice would you give to someone thinking about opening or expanding a child care center?

Probably the most important advice when starting a center is to be well capitalized. You will always spend way more than you thought and that's usually where a lot of people get in trouble.

Thoughts from Sholom:

You can't manage what you can't measure. The company should always have metrics to help everyone know how they're progressing towards your mission.

CHILD CARE PROFILE

Lisa Fromen

Children's Ark Academy

Location: Georgia
Year Opened: 2006
# of Employees: 22
# of Locations: 1
2017 Gross Revenue: $1,014,689

How did you finance your first location and what did it cost?

My first school I purchased in Florida 23 years ago. I had absolutely no money but I had the belief that I could figure it out. I found a school that would owner finance me so I took out all the cash advances I could off my credit cards for a down payment and bought my first school in 1996. After I establishing myself I took out a loan to pay off the credit card debt so the interest rate was more reasonable. I paid the debt off of the school loan and credit card loan off within 6 years. I was offered cash for my school in 2006. I didn't have much overhead so my school of capacity of 74 that I had for 10 years left me with a savings of about 200,000.00. I purchased my second school in Georgia in 2006. Here is where I have made most of my mistakes.

What was the biggest mistake you made in your business in the first two years?

Initial mistake was through the bank record before I purchased the school. I didn't live in Georgia so I didn't really get to see if the school actually had the children in attendance. After the school was purchased I found out that the owner's children were putting money into the school's bank account to make it look like the school was profitable. So now my $18,000 mortgage sucked all my savings out the first 90 days. Being a single unmarried owner for the last 4 years has been really hard. I really believe that if I knew then what I know now that I have learned through Kris Murray and the Child Care Success Academy in 2006 it wouldn't have taken me as long as it has to build it back up.

What are some of the smartest business decisions you have ever made?

I have the tendency to give people many chances to redeem themselves but learning that it is better to let staff go immediately when it isn't a good fit is better in the long run. I was on my way to creating a management team that I thought would allow me to work more on my business then in it and I hired an Executive Director the summer of 2017 to add to my team of a director and assistant director filling in the gaps of my current management teams' weaknesses. The new Executive Director in so many words made a mess of things and I had to let her go even though my current director of 9 years quit in the middle of the mess. Even though I had no director and at the time the assistant director was gone because of a death in the family it was the best business decision I had ever made even though it was a scary thing to do at the time.

What advice would you give to someone thinking about opening or expanding a child care center?

I think that building a great trustworthy management team is crucial. It is very difficult to move forward by yourself. I think also cross training other people to step in is also very important.

Thoughts from Lisa:

She is clothed with strength and dignity and she laughs without fear of the future. Proverbs 31:25.

Chapter 7
Expansion

Child care businesses are very susceptible to economic downturns. When moms and dads start losing their jobs and unemployment rises, child care is one of the first things a parent eliminates.

Once kids start leaving your center, it becomes a waterfall effect and it happens very quickly. I can remember vividly in 2007 having a record year, and by the end of 2008 we had lost about 35% of our children.

Why on Earth would I pick an economic downturn to start expanding my business? Simple physics, what goes down must come up. If I could buy existing centers for pennies on the dollar when times were tough, and things were at their worst, I knew that when things improved I would have amazing lease terms, and a very profitable center.

In 2007 when the economy was booming I was looking to expand. I had 3 locations at that point and had the largest child care center chain in Maine. I sent a letter out to all of the competitors in my area letting them know a couple things.

- I was possibly interested in buying them out.
- I had plans to expand, possibly right in their neighborhood.
- I would take good care of their staff and parents.
- I do not deal with business brokers, so they would have to call me directly if interested.

Do not do a deal for the sake of adding locations. Always be willing to walk away from a deal if something does not seem right. I have clients that I work with that have overpaid for their building or for the business and when enrollment drops they are in financial trouble. Do smart deals!

In this chapter I will give you 10 nuggets as a starting point on how to start the process of expanding your business. These nuggets will act as a teaser for you, as I am already working on my next book which will be all about child care expansion. Please feel free contact me at brian@childcaremillionaire.com if you need help with your expansion plans, we have several expansion specialists on staff.

NUGGET #90:
It All Starts with a Decision to Expand

You have made the decision to expand your business, now what? A million questions come flooding into your mind. The stress starts to build and then panic sets in. I have been there many times.

I have clients ask me all of the time what they should do next when it comes to expansion, and the first step is to examine where you are now.

Whether you are a home provider for seven children in the Bronx or a single center owner licensed for 150 in Texas, both of you want to expand, but your ideas of expansion are going to be totally different!

Start by sitting down and writing all of the reasons why you want to expand. Make a long list of pros and cons and use that to help you make the decision on the timing of when you would like to begin the process.

If you are still reading I am assuming you are interested in some type of expansion - good for you! It is up to you to figure out what that looks like, and I will give you some tips over the next few nuggets to help you start to figure out a plan for getting you there.

NUGGET #91:
Systemize Everything

Go into any McDonald's in the world and they are all pretty much run the same way. Why? Systems.

To properly expand your business successfully you need to be able to create duplicatable systems that allow you to basically duplicate your brand, culture and marketing over and over again.

It is much less expensive to use the same branding and company name in each new location you open, but you must be able to have systems in place to ensure that as you expand it is seamless. If you were able to take an employee from an existing location and move them on day one of a new center this person should know exactly what to do and where to go for answers because there are systems in place.

An operations manual is a great way to systematize everything. A video training library can help as well. Make sure each employee knows how to access answers to any possible question or scenario that may arise.

The more you can replicate your new location based off of your existing one, the easier and less stressful it will be to grow to a large operation.

NUGGET #92:
Ensure You are Properly Capitalized

It takes money to make money and child care expansion is no exception. Although I have opened locations with very little money, I am the exception and not the rule.

Expansion can be the worst thing you have ever done with your business if you do it wrong and the best thing you could ever do if you do it right.

In many of the previous nuggets I have given you financial advice on how to build up reserves and reduce debt. This is key to expansion since you need to make sure you are in a proper financial position to do so. Expansion without proper capitalization can bankrupt you.

You are excited about expanding and find a new building to open a child care center. They want $10,000 a month and you think that is reasonable since you worked the numbers in your head and think that you can get a license for 100 children and you can make $100,000 in annual profit if you were full.

The problem is you never start full, and there is no guarantee you will make a profit in the first year. If enrollment is slow for the first six months (timing is everything) can you still pay the rent, electric, sewer, payroll, water, insurance, gas, and maintenance costs?

When you have to start robbing profits from your other location to pay ongoing expenses for a new location, you are on the downward slide to taking your whole business down. Being properly funded from day one will help to avoid this.

I recommend making sure you have at least six months' worth of full operating expenses in the bank as working capital to fund the expansion of a new location. I also recommend not taking any profits out of a new location until the money that you used for working capital is paid back in full to your savings account for your next expansion.

I know you can borrow from a bank for working capital, but I do not recommend this unless you have to. If you cannot save up for this, you are not ready to properly expand. You will work harder to make your new center be successful if you know that YOUR money is invested in it, not the banks.

NUGGET #93:
Creative Financing

There are many ways to finance an expansion, and I have personally done it a variety of ways. I do not think one way is necessarily better than the other but do consider your personal situation when deciding how to finance your expansion.

Proper capitalization is vital. The proper amount is much more important than the source of the funds.

Most owners start at a bank when they want to expand. The owner walks in and tells the loan officer they would like to borrow money to expand their business. This becomes day one of a sixty-day financial colonoscopy to determine your creditworthiness.

I have never borrowed from a bank to expand my business, I never had to. I found other creative ways to do so and I am going to share them with you in this nugget.

My first location that I expanded to out of my home daycare was funded by my best friend Joel Billings. I had no money and I asked him to borrow $5,000 and he did not hesitate and got a cash advance on his credit card for me. This allowed me to put a fire system in my church to open my first center. So, consider borrowing from friends and family, and consider making them investors so they can share in some of the profits.

My second center I used owner financing to give me the startup capital to open. I worked a deal with the landlord to give me $25,000 worth of working capital in exchange for a 5-year lease on his building. He enjoyed doing business with me so much that he bought my third location for me and leased it back to me for no money down.

After I had three locations I started getting a bit cocky. I wanted to dominate my market, so I sent letters out to all of my competitors asking them if they wanted to sell, and if they did to make sure they contacted me first.

One of those competitors actually reached out to me because they were interested in selling. I looked at all of the financials and did my due diligence, but I did not like the $250,000 price tag on the business (no real estate). I turned the deal down.

My fourth center was another scenario where I had to put no money down and was able to walk in and start making profits from day one. A local hospital about 30 minutes away called and wanted us to run a child care center adjacent to the hospital. The CEO had heard of this letter I sent out and thought we would be a good fit. They bought us the building and renovated it to our specs and then leased it back to us for zero upfront cost.

Then, when one of our competitors was closing, we started getting phone calls from their frustrated parents that needed immediate care for their children. We immediately approached them about taking over and started negotiations. We did expedited due diligence and found substantial tax liens on the business so we did not want to take the risk. We let them close, negotiated a lease with the landlord, and bought all of the daycare equipment at auction from the bank for pennies on the dollar. All in all, this location cost me $10,000 and it has generated over $4 million in revenue over the last 12 years.

Location number six was a result of the letter I sent out a year before. I was approached by a gentleman who wanted out of the child care business. We negotiated a deal where I walked in for zero money down and I got all of his equipment for nothing. I did a five-year lease and gave him a small percentage of the profits for five years. I bought the building from him two years ago and this has been a profitable location for me.

Location number seven approached us a year after the letter was sent out. It was a church daycare that was down the road from one of my other schools. She only wanted $7,000 for the business and all equipment. The center was small, but profitable. I wrote a check and took it over. We were there three years and had major issues with the church leadership, so we did not renew our lease at this location.

Location number eight was a result of the location that I previously discussed that I turned down two years earlier who wanted too much money. They were desperate to sell and wanted $70,000 for the location. By this time, I was doing very good financially and wrote a check and paid in cash for the business. I bought the building from the landlord (no money down, owner financing) and this location is very profitable today.

Location number nine is the same as location number seven. The church went bankrupt and put the building on the market and we bought the building. The man that I bought location number eight from purchased the property and owner financed the building for me, all for no money down at a very attractive interest rate.

So, you can see I have done many different finance options but have never been to a bank. I am a firm believer if there is a will there's a way. I had very little money for my first few expansions, so I had to be creative. As I grew I still used creative financing as I thought it was a better fit for me. You have to decide what type of financing is best for you.

Other financing considerations:

- Retirement Savings Account

- Roll Over Business Startup (ROBS)
- Small Business Administration (SBA)
- Bank or Credit Union
- Friend or Relative
- Personal Savings
- Credit Cards
- Home Equity Line of Credit
- Venture Capitalist
- Investor
- Owner Financing

It does not matter how you decide to finance your new center, it is up to you. The secret is to find a way and do not accept no as an answer. Keep these 10 expansion nuggets in mind and you should be in good shape. Don't forget to drop me a note at brian@childcaremillionaire.com and let me in on your creative financing methods for expanding to a new center.

NUGGET #94:
Have a Warrior Mindset

It takes a warrior mindset to expand your center profitably. The letter I sent out that led to several of my locations was a clear example of a warrior mindset.

You must be willing to do what others won't to be able to have what others cannot. The easy way to expand is to simply go to the internet and look at the for-sale listing with a broker who has over inflated the price. It is another thing to go out and talk someone into selling their business at a below retail price without having to pay a broker commission.

Someone with warrior mindset is always looking for a good deal, and never pays retail. He or she is a great negotiator and is very patient, always willing to walk away from a deal. He or she is goal driven and very focused.

The better deal you get, the quicker the center will be profitable and the less chance that the center will fail. Since profits are usually always the lead motivator behind expansion, this will help you get there much quicker. Put on your suit of armor and go into battle armed with knowledge, patience, passion, capital, and experience and you will dominate your market.

NUGGET #95:
Be the Big Fish in the Small Pond

As I started to expand I was faced with the question of how I wanted to expand. I could either put one large center in each geographical area, or I could choose to put several medium sized centers spread out around the city, with no city resident having to drive more than 2 miles to reach one of my locations.

I chose to dominate my market and offer convenience to my customers at the same time. You may think that if you live in a metropolitan area this does not apply to you - if you think that you are wrong.

Dominating a market has to do with brand recognition. In my city I can honestly say there is not one family that has not heard of our program. This is how you dominate your market.

Because I have centers throughout my city I have children changing locations all of the time. When a parent changes jobs, they can transfer without an issue to one of my other locations. The same goes for employees. We are able to shuffle them between locations to save payroll expenses and reduce overstaffing.

Before you try to put your second location an hour away, first look 10 minutes away. It will be a whole lot easier to run a closer school and you will start becoming the big fish in the small pond. Once everyone in your city knows you, marketing dollars get more bang for the buck and you don't have to spend as many of them.

NUGGET #96:
Think Outside of the Box

As you begin looking for locations to put a child care center you really need to start thinking outside the box.

I currently own two churches that most people would not consider when looking for real estate to purchase for a child care center.

Churches are an incredible investment for a child care center. Why? The real estate price is always way below market, normally they have open floor plans and classrooms already set up, plus many have ample outside play area.

I have seen centers open up in former restaurants, banks, strip malls, shopping malls, fraternity halls, schools, and office complexes.

As long as the zoning will allow, you can put a center anywhere there are people willing to drive to. Very seldom will the former use deter people from bringing their children, except maybe a former funeral home or strip club.

Once you have it in your mind that you will look where others won't, you are well on the way to having a warrior mindset.

NUGGET #97:
Use Brokers to Sell, but Not Necessarily to Buy

I spent many years as a real estate agent when I left the U.S. Navy, so I know firsthand all about the real estate market.

A business broker's job is to sell his client's property for as much money as humanly possible to collect the biggest possible commission. If you are a seller, you want a good broker on your side.

In my line of work as a certified child care coach I have met a dozen or so brokers, some of them are amazing. I have also met others who have lost their way in the pursuit of profits and notoriety.

To know whether or not you have found a good brokerage firm, first look at what they do for their clients. Is child care brokerage all that they do? Is that what they specialize in? Are they 100% committed to selling your school when it is listed or has their business and their focus been taken off selling your school for the best price? Your first question to ask the broker is if child care buying and selling is 100% their focus, and if the answer is yes you can proceed with them.

I have purchased many schools, and I have never used a broker. If I did I would never have found the deals that I did. I'll never know if I possibly missed a great deal by not having one. What I am trying to say is no one ever sells a non-performing school with a broker. Non-performing schools are all I am interested in buying because they have the potential for the most profit.

If you ever decide that you are ready to sell, I recommend calling the best broker you can find. A center that is 85% full or better for the previous two years will sell for the best price.

NUGGET #98:
Study the Competition

When you are in expansion mode make sure to study how your competitors have expanded. In my market I am the only multi-site owner, so I did the opposite of everyone else.

Does anyone dominate your market? What is the average size of new schools being built? How elaborate are the new schools being built? Are centers full with waiting lists in your market? What is everyone charging for tuition? Are there big box franchise schools being built? What are the centers that are expanding paying staff members?

Doing your homework by knowing answers to all of these questions can help you decide on where and when to expand. The more opposition research you can do the better you will be at looking for opportunities others have missed.

I have a client who owns six locations in New England. She was so excited years ago when a major national preschool chain was being built across the street from one of her locations. Most of you would probably fear this. I asked her why this excited her. She told me she knew they would be spending a boatload of money in advertising to get people to tour the school, and they would see her location and tour it as well. She knew her program was better and more affordable. Two years later, she was still in business and they weren't. Mindset is everything, believe in your program and know your competition inside and out.

NUGGET #99:
Five Centers Are Easier to Manage Than One

Running one center is one of the hardest jobs on the planet, in my opinion.

I have many clients who own only one school, and overall, they work much harder and are way more stressed than my clients with five or more centers. Plus, they usually make a whole lot less money. Working harder for less money and more stress is usually not an attractive option.

Why don't people expand from one location to five? Because most single site owners feel that five locations will yield five times the work, stress, and aggravation and that is simply not true if done properly.

The benefit of having multiple schools is the power of delegation. Due to physics and the fact that you can only be in one place at a time, you are forced to delegate and put systems in place to run schools without you having to be there to make every little decision.

Once you have those systems in place, and can trust your people, you can now spend time working on your business instead of in your business and you will be able to relax more and take more vacations.

NUGGET #100:
Patience is Key

Never be rushed into any deal. Make sure you always take your time and do proper due diligence on each and every possible deal.

Always be willing to walk away from a deal. Having this mindset will allow you to have all of the power. The one with the power is the one who always gets the best deal.

I wish you the best of luck with your expansion, and if you would like to discuss your expansion plans with me please visit http://www.childcaremillionaire.com and sign up for a complimentary strategy session. I truly hope to have the opportunity to meet you!

NUGGET #101:

Recommended Reading

This is a list of some amazing books that I highly recommend reading. Since my list is always evolving, please visit my website at http://www.childcaremillionaire.com to see my latest recommendations. You can actually order each of the books below (and also any book on Amazon.com) by visiting my website. 100% of the profits generated from ordering a book from my website will go to the Make a Wish Foundation.

Amazing Child Care Books:

- The Ultimate Child Care Marketing Guide – Kris Murray
- The 77 Best Strategies to Grow your Early Childhood Program – Kris Murray
- Relationship Roadmap: Real World Strategies for Cultivating a Positive and Collaborative Culture in Your Preschool - Sindye Alexander
- Don't Go! A Practical Guide for Tackling Employee Turnover —Vernon H. Mason, Jr. M.Ed.
- Get Out! But Before You Go…. Practical Steps to Turn Your Zero into a Hero or Set Them Free! —Vernon H. Mason, Jr. M.Ed.

Leadership & Mindset Books by Dr. John Maxwell:

- Developing the Leaders Around You
- Developing the Leader Within You
- Put Your Dream to the Test
- Sometimes You Win, Sometimes You Learn
- The 21 Irrefutable Laws of Leadership
- Today Matters
- Intentional Living
- The 360 Degree Leader
- The 17 Essential Qualities of a Team Player
- The 21 Indispensable Qualities of a Leader
- Becoming a Person of Influence
- Failing Forward

Financial Books by Robert Kiyosaki:

- Rich Dad Poor Dad
- The Cash Flow Quadrant
- Real Estate Riches

Motivational Books by other authors I like:

- The Slight Edge – Jeff Olson
- The Bible – God
- Leaders Eat Last – Simon Sinek
- Start with Why - Simon Sinek
- Driving Leaders – Chris Cappy
- Traction – Gino Wickman
- The 7 Habits of Highly Effective People – Stephen Covey
- Awaken the Giant Within – Anthony Robbins
- The Power of Positive Thinking – Norman Vincent Peale
- What Got You Here Won't Get You There – Marshall Goldsmith

Made in the USA
Monee, IL
27 July 2020